CAMBRIDGE MUSIC HANDBOOKS

Holst: *The Planets*

CAMBRIDGE MUSIC HANDBOOKS

GENERAL EDITOR Julian Rushton

Cambridge Music Handbooks provide accessible introductions to major musical works, written by the most informed commentators in the field.

With the concert-goer, performer and student in mind, the books present essential information on the historical and musical context, the composition, and the performance and reception history of each work, or group of works, as well as critical discussion of the music.

Other published titles

Bach: The Brandenburg Concertos MALCOLM BOYD
Bach: Mass in B Minor JOHN BUTT
Beethoven: *Missa solemnis* WILLIAM DRABKIN
Beethoven: Symphony No. 9 NICHOLAS COOK
Berg: Violin Concerto ANTHONY POPLE
Berlioz: *Roméo et Juliette* JULIAN RUSHTON
Chopin: The Four Ballades JIM SAMSON
Debussy: *La mer* SIMON TREZISE
Handel: *Messiah* DONALD BURROWS
Haydn: *The Creation* NICHOLAS TEMPERLEY
Haydn: String Quartets, Op. 50 W. DEAN SUTCLIFFE
Janáček: *Glagolitic Mass* PAUL WINGFIELD
Mahler: Symphony No. 3 PETER FRANKLIN
Mendelssohn: *The Hebrides* and other overtures R. LARRY TODD
Mozart: The 'Jupiter' Symphony ELAINE SISMAN
Musorgsky: *Pictures at an Exhibition* MICHAEL RUSS
Schoenberg: *Pierrot lunaire* JONATHAN DUNSBY
Schubert: *Die schöne Müllerin* SUSAN YOUENS
Schumann: Fantasie, Op. 17 NICHOLAS MARSTON
Sibelius: Symphony No. 5 JAMES HEPOKOSKI
Strauss: *Also sprach Zarathustra* JOHN WILLIAMSON
Stravinsky: *Oedipus rex* STEPHEN WALSH

Holst: *The Planets*

Richard Greene
Loyola College of Music
New Orleans

CAMBRIDGE UNIVERSITY PRESS
Cambridge, New York, Melbourne, Madrid, Cape Town, Singapore, São Paulo

Cambridge University Press
The Edinburgh Building, Cambridge CB2 2RU, UK

Published in the United States of America by Cambridge University Press, New York

www.cambridge.org
Information on this title: www.cambridge.org/9780521450003

First published 1995

A catalogue record for this publication is available from the British Library

Library of Congress Cataloguing in Publication data
Greene, Richard.
Holst, The planets / Richard Greene.
p. cm. – (Cambridge music handbooks)
Includes bibliographical references (p.) and index.
ISBN 0 521 45000 4 (hardback). – ISBN 0 521 45633 9 (paperback)
1. Holst, Gustav, 1874–1934. Planets. I. Title. II. Title: Planets. III. Series.
ML410.H748G74 1995
784.2'1858–dc20 94–17175 CIP MN

ISBN-13 978-0-521-45000-3 hardback
ISBN-10 0-521-45000-4 hardback

ISBN-13 978-0-521-45633-3 paperback
ISBN-10 0-521-45633-9 paperback

Transferred to digital printing 2006

To Beth, Parks, and Grace

Contents

Acknowledgements

I would like to thank the following for their assistance and support: Loyola University, New Orleans, for granting me the academic leave during which much of my research was done; Lowinger Maddison (Honorary Curator of the Archive at The Holst Birthplace Museum) and Sophie Wilson (Cheltenham Museum System) for accommodating me beyond the call of duty; Dr. John Murphy (Loyola University) for his comments on the introduction; and Penny Souster and the staff of Cambridge University Press for making this project possible. A special thanks to Professor Julian Rushton, whose patience, expertise, and vision have guided me throughout the writing of this book.

Introduction

Gustav Holst was born on 21 September 1874, under the sign of Virgo, ruled by the planet Mercury.

Mercury, as Holst would have read in his copy of Alan Leo's *What Is a Horoscope and How Is It Cast?*, is known as the "winged messenger of the gods," and a favorable planet for those who have left the senses for the mind. It is a mutable planet, absorbing all with which it comes into contact. Since Holst's death in 1934, those who knew him and who have written about him have given witness – though perhaps unwittingly – to his Mercurian attributes. There is always accent upon his mental life; physically frail and prone to illness, he was indefatigable in his curiosity and intellectual flights. His was not a brilliant personality, making him once again, according to the descriptions in Leo's book, a typical Mercurian; nor was he ever interested, compositionally, in fluency and pyrotechnics for their own sake. Slow and plodding in his work habits, he was often criticized late in his life for lacking spontaneity, for being too mechanical and dry. Early in his professional career, he fell into school teaching – the young ladies at St. Paul's Girls' School and, at Morley College, the working class – as a way to support his family. And this daily school work may well have contributed to his methodical ways, and might have played a part in the development of a technique which found beauty and cleverness in simple musical devices. But his schedule would have been exhausting and often tedious, giving him little scope and virtually no time for his own development as a serious composer.

But, on 15 November 1920, at Queen's Hall, London, there erupted a work by this seemingly dull and limited school teacher, composed in his spare time, which dazzled both music critics and audiences alike in a way not felt on English soil since Elgar's *Enigma Variations*; a work which continues to attract listeners today.

If the gap between Holst, as we *thought* we knew him, and this most vibrant of musical compositions seems too great, we have in part our historical mentality to blame; a mentality which gropes for firm watersheds and beacons

1

to lead the way forward. The history of *The Planets* as a musical force is, like Holst's life, filled with unexpected twists; and, like its composer, it fell victim to notoriety when it needed a more sensitive hearing. Holst's close friend and collaborator, the writer Clifford Bax, described the composer – in 1914, the year that *The Planets* was begun – as an apparent failure.[1] Yet, by 1914 there had been over forty public performances of his works (not counting various school concerts), many in London, with a number of pieces receiving repeat performances – this last feat being somewhat unusual for a young British composer. How is failure defined in the face of such apparent success? If Holst can be said to have been a failure, it would have been in his lack of works in "important" genres – symphonies, string quartets and others which were the foundation of the German "masterwork" tradition. Furthermore, those of his compositions which stemmed from nineteenth-century German practice did not project a distinctive, original "voice." So the young composer, in the eyes of the critics, either failed to establish a place among the "best" (i.e. the German) composers, or he ignored those influences. His partsongs and folkloric works were English, and therefore of lesser stature in critical circles; his compositions based on Hindu scales and religious texts (the so-called "Sanskrit" works) were curious and original, but too far afield in their materials and rhetoric to find a place in serious musical discussions.

With *The Planets* there was no longer any doubt, for the English listener at any rate, as to Holst's success. His victory was both musical and political in that it represented a substantial relationship with the English audience as well as with reviewers and critics. In this work he was able to speak clearly and deeply to his audience, and the sense of authority projected by it moved them to trust in his musicianship. Likewise, his "language" – his musical materials and the various ways of relating and elaborating them – was consistent enough under the great variety of styles and characters to convince the critics of the composer's ability. But perhaps most important is the fact that Holst had found a way of using the conventions of nineteenth-century European music as a context for his own particular style, linking himself, finally, to the traditions esteemed so highly by the English musical community.

But in this success there is paradox, even irony. *The Planets* is both one of the most recognized, while at the same time one of the least known, works in the standard orchestral repertoire. Often spoken of – and certainly intended – as a single entity, it has been most often heard, and remembered, in fragments. Since Holst's death the work has remained critically ignored while parts of it have entered into the general cultural repository of musical signs. Such notoriety can be as much a curse as a blessing. For *The Planets*, it results in a less than critical hearing, and the work loses its richness of character for the listener. It is only with a complete performance, and with a hearing which honors what the music itself has to say, that we can begin to fathom the work as a personal statement by this enigmatic composer.

The curious mixture of critical failure and popular success which characterizes the reception of *The Planets* points to the difference between critics and general listeners where new music was concerned. It seems paradoxical that a composition which has genuinely moved audiences for well over half a century could not be musically strong; yet the aesthetic stance of many critics – then as now – worked against a favorable hearing of the piece. The musical ideal, as articulated by such critics, and stemming from late nineteenth-century German discussions on the topic, was for a musical composition to exist as a pure structure – every note working in relation to all others in establishing a meaningful, though abstract, form. This ideal was based on a particular reading of the music of the great German symphonic tradition; programmatic music was a lesser art since it relied on ideas and statements outside of the musical structure. Likewise, any music the form of which could not be fixed within the structural tradition of the ideal was suspect. *The Planets*, in spite of its initial success with reviewers, was resistant to accepted analytical approaches. The structures of individual movements were loose and rambling; the musical progression was lacking in Beethovenian-style development; tonal grammar was difficult to hierarchize. Repeated attempts to discuss the work made it seem totally dependent on the titles and subtitles – its program.

Yet the fact remains: the music continues to excite listeners. The implication is that there was (and is) a strong musical experience which was resistant to traditional analysis and structural theory as they existed at the time. Furthermore, *The Planets*, and perhaps many similar works written in this century, can be seen to be governed by principles extending beyond German structuralist approaches. Had more sensitive analytical systems existed which could have explained how these pieces worked as musical communications, it is likely that they would have fared better in European critical circles. This book develops one such theory, which requires the old distinction between program music and abstract music to be reconsidered, and new concepts – musical metaphor, evolving structures and the like – to be developed. The basic structures and relationships of the music would take on rhetorical functions; in other words, rather than existing for themselves, they would work as part of a human communication. With such an analytical system, Holst's music speaks for itself, and we are able to hear what it has to say.

Musical character and a theory of musical rhetoric

To speak of what the music itself has to say means to allow the musical action to communicate with us. This is an analytical issue, but not simply in the sense of parsing and classifying and judging against a textbook standard. While Holst compared himself to a mathematician working through a problem, he also was convinced that music should be a communication from composer to listener. He also felt that music could, in fact, speak for itself, without the help of program notes. *The Planets* was to make its appeal to the audience without any explanation from the composer. It was a series of "mood pictures," he was to say in a lecture some years after the piece was premièred, with the movements acting as foils for one another. They were to be "embodiments" of the characters suggested by their subtitles. At the same time, he did not consider them program music – they imitated no real-world event or personality, they narrated no extra-musical plot. This distinction between communication and program is at the heart of the analytical issue, and it brings the discussion into the realm of rhetoric, the craft of expressive communication.

The titles and subtitles of *The Planets* were not, for the composer, a programmatic touch; they were metaphors. That is to say, as in literary theory, they embodied character through the action of some agent not naturally associated with it. In music, this agent would be the actions embodied in the materials of the particular composition. There are some programmatic touches in *The Planets*, for example the snare-drum cadence and the trumpet fanfares in *Mars* imitating the sounds of an army going into battle. But *Mars* does not narrate a particular battle; rather, the musical events – the chromatic in-flections and ramblings, the insistent but unconventional rhythmic figures – act as metaphors of the emotive and psychological states which we associate with the idea of war. In other words, there is an actual battle taking place within the abstract world of the music, a war on its own terms, not those of the real world; and our attention to that struggle invokes in us, the listeners, a vicarious response and an understanding of the parallels between the world of the music and our own.

Of course, Holst was not the first to use musical figures or style to project character or to represent some real-world condition. By the time *The Planets* was composed, there was already a longstanding tradition of musical rhetoric of which Strauss's programmatic works can be considered only the most exaggerated examples. In the symphonic tradition of the eighteenth and nineteenth centuries, the repository of topical associations – of styles and figures linked to social status and activities, religion, military life and the like – was very large indeed, and we can see in the works of the most respected composers of the era – Haydn, Mozart, Beethoven, and then Schubert and Schumann – how their treatment of topical idioms might have directed and enhanced their communication with an audience.[2] The use of topics would have created a link for the audience between the music and the outside world; yet the music would not be considered programmatic, as the topics acted as metaphors rather than depictions of real-world situations. The concept of topic can also be used to demonstrate the rhetorical "problem" faced by these composers: their music was often filled with too varied a range of materials and treatments within a single piece for the audience to conceive the music as integrated, and therefore meaningful. By juxtaposing topical gestures chock-a-block, and by altering them unexpectedly or in ways considered inappropriate by the audience, the composers pushed metaphor to its limits, forcing the listener to go against intuition and conventional experience. Resolution to a minor chord, for example, said something with reference to the apparent darkness of the chord and the feel of "solution" and "resolution," and, metaphorically, about the topic with which it was associated. In other words, the relative quality and feel of chord, mode, key relations, rhythmic character, or whatever else was used, said something about the topic which appears in the musical context, and the relative difficulty or dissonance exhibited becomes, through metaphor, part of the unique character given to the topic. In the late works of Mozart and Beethoven the greatly distended sense of various topics and the unconventional treatment of them were likely causes of the confusion with which the music was first met.

With Schubert and Schumann, and those who followed them, the process began to involve more personal associations and more individual formulations of topical idiom. But the process of metaphorizing remained essentially the same; and when Wagner stated that every part and detail of the music was to be an original idea or the consequence of an original idea as music took on a "truth function," he was recommissioning metaphor as the essential artistic function.[3]

Holst's musical rhetoric can be seen as an outgrowth of this tradition, particularly through his early affinity for Wagnerian harmony and melodic grammar, seen in such works as *The Mystic Trumpeter* (1904) and *The Cloud Messenger* (1913). But it was also through that nineteenth-century model that he came into contact with a quite different source, Symbolist theory. The chief proponent of Symbolist concepts in music was Debussy, and after him, Skryabin, both of whom were well known to London audiences. For Debussy, the Symbolists' use of words as "open" metaphors led to an affective representation which was a model for his intuitive and grammatically free musical constructions. Likewise, Wagner's *leitmotif* system, as a means of organizing both emotive plot and musical development, parallels (indeed, was a source for) Symbolist concepts.[4] A study of the processes in Holst's music, in conjunction with his verbal clues, demonstrates the Symbolist model clearly.[5] One example is his affinity for embedding compositions within a distancing "frame," which reflects a rhetorical outlook similar to Debussy's, although the musical materials may have differed. Many of the Sanskrit works (such as the opera *Savitri* [1908] and the *Choral Hymns from the Rig Veda* [1908–12]), as well as the mystical *Planets*, *Venus* and *Neptune*, project this idea, but purportedly non-mystical works make use of it as well: *A Somerset Rhapsody* (1906–7), the third movement of *Beni Mora* (1909–10), *Saturn*, *The Choral Symphony* (1925), *Egdon Heath* (1927), *Hammersmith* (1931), and the *Lyric Movement* (1933), to name the important works.[6] These compositions all begin with such quiet, often monophonic expressions that the silence from which they emerge is palpable. The openings remove the rest of the piece from the everyday world and guide the listener to a recognizable but utterly separate world within. This device allowed Holst to use conventional musical symbols in new ways and, particularly, to use prosaic material – silly dance tunes and awkward, rough-cut gestures – to poetic (which is to say, metaphoric) ends. The frame allowed all within it to be subject to transformation, including genre itself, and all aspects of the music functioned as metaphor.

Seen in this light, musical character is not simply the result of fixed associations with the physical world. When purposefully chosen musical gestures are set in purposeful relationships with one another, musical character can be said to arise. The connection with the "real world" – the program – will be developed only as a jumping-off place into the separate world of the music. Such a strategy is in keeping with literary theory of the day – for example, in the essays of E. M. Forster and Henry James – which emphasizes the importance of a character's structural function over an imitative one. James discusses the need to keep some of his characters superficial so that they will not detract from more important aspects of his plot, and even his main characters will be stripped of all but those features which are necessary to the unfolding of their stories. Such a relationship between character and structure gives a story a stronger sense of reality and individuality, even if the plot follows conventional lines. This provides the final point in Holst's method, the relationship between structure and character. Ultimately, an appreciation of musical character requires that it be understood as the natural result of *musical action*, and the listener's perception of that action.

Such actions need to be controlled and guided by a structure, specifically one which arises from the particulars of the musical characters themselves. Thus, musical gestures – rhythmic, melodic, harmonic and others – are not dropped into a pre-existent form; rather, the structure evolves out of their musical (as opposed to real-world) qualities, just as a literary plot is derived from its characters (as opposed to "real persons") and their propensities. Holst was quite clear on this point. He considered form not tied to content as "cold storage"; and formal analysis was "quite interesting and not dangerous as long as you do not imagine that it has any direct bearing on Art."[7] Ultimately, expressive power is based on the *sensitivity* as well as on the strength of the structure. In Holst's case, his control was far greater than the aesthetic product at first suggests, though his critics often found him too calculating. With regard to *The Planets*, his audience's response was a far stronger witness to the efficacy of both his structures and his rhetoric.

Always practical, Holst tried to match a systemic rigor with rhetorical immediacy, and it was common, with his late works, to find critics admitting that the composer had said exactly what he meant to say but that they themselves were unable to find words to express it. This situation was often explained by invoking "intuition," yet Holst's work-a-day methods suggest otherwise. The composer's approach was easily construed as intuitive because the listener was induced to establish the proper context for interpreting the music without attention being called to the fact. For example, in *The Planets* it is the unusual tonal and formal situations one encounters from the very beginning which invoke the necessary nineteenth-century conventions simply by breaking the rules so obviously. In a late work such as *Egdon Heath* (1927), the same is true: the opening line follows a tortured tonal/modal path while being organized at a higher, but still perceivable, level around the conventional tonic–dominant polarity. These events are not announced within the rhetoric expected of tonal music, and so they make their mark subliminally. Furthermore, Holst began to make allusions to his own personal style, his own way of dealing with current "topics." This results in such stylistic allusions as "folk" and "varieties," and personal feelings concerning the mystical or ecstatic states being perceived by the astute listener without overt extra-musical images coming to mind. This is certainly suggested by a reading of reviewers' comments; they consistently maintain a narrow range of metaphor, while pronouncing the music unfathomable.

By starting from the implied – and perhaps we can say intuited – metaphors, it is possible to follow the expansive and emotive journey embodied by *The Planets*, from the *physical*, *aggressive* and *profligate* to the *mystical*, *passive* and *stoic* experience which lingers as the final strains of *Neptune* evaporate in space around us. The analysis which unfolds in the following chapters will demonstrate that the music does not simply provide "signs" of these states of being; rather, it projects a formal progression which, when placed against nineteenth-century conventions, yields the sense of those states. A nineteenth-century context is assumed because of Holst's background and environment and because of the formal and tonal evidence within the music. The piece is discussed in psychological terms rather than standard programmatic terms because the interpretive experience is based less on the objective result of the music and more on the listener's inner struggle to synthesize events and a convention which accounts for all of the musical action.

Is Holst's conception in *The Planets*, then, one of human psychological phases? There is a striking similarity of outlook between Holst and his *Planets*, as we hear them proceed. Each movement can be held up against Holst's life as a mirror: the rigid lock-step of his over-scheduled life was an oppressive ordeal for him, leading ultimately to a nervous breakdown; but the peacefulness of love, of human relationships, while comforting and beautiful, was essentially inert and non-productive. The fleet-footedness of his mind and its restless fancy was a welcome universe which bore fruit, and it led to great celebration, physical and energizing. At the same time, Holst had a great preoccupation with an acceptance of one's destiny, and it led to a cultivation of a stoicism which left him apparently insensitive and cold. The paradox is that such a state of mind could exist side by side with the tomfoolery of *Uranus*, but ultimately all gives way before the mystical state which the composer apparently sought continually in the act of composition. This seemingly passive state was not inert for him, nor anti-intellectual; its summing up of all the threads of life in a single conceptualization was an annihilation of physical time and space. It granted him, perhaps, such vision that it was worth the loss of reputation and popularity which he was to sustain in later life.

1

Holst and the two Londons

When Gustav Holst came up to London from the West Country in 1893, he entered a world far removed from provincial life. There were, perhaps, always two Londons for the young Holst: the rather formal environment of the Royal College of Music and the kaleidoscopic world of Hammersmith where he lodged as a student. The first concentrated him on serious music and the past; Charles Villiers Stanford, his composition teacher at the College, enclosed his students in a worldview culminating in the music of Brahms.[1] The second world was filled with a happy and perhaps vulgar culture; music halls, varieties and all forms of popular music. He appears to have happily kept a foot in both camps, for the two worlds are often found side by side in his music, and the tension between the two was a fundamental influence as the composer forged his personal style.

These two worlds were, in reality, but two aspects of Victorian London, highbrow and lowbrow. Edwardian London, with its rising middle class, was characterized by a merging of these two cultural strains, giving birth to a well-crafted popular style and the potential for the language of the folktune and the sentimental ballad to be molded into a more intense and serious artistic statement.

There was a gap of seven years between the time Holst began work on *The Planets* and the first public performance in 1920, meaning that it was conceived in a London clinging to a fast fading Edwardian spirit, but born and raised in the new world of post-war Europe. It can be argued that the work owes its peculiar amalgamation of styles and idioms to the way in which Holst lived his life in the earlier period and to the city's influence on him. Yet it is equally true that the work owes its success to the greater openness and stronger passions of what was eventually to be called the Jazz Age.

London before the war

By 1913, the classical music scene in London was quite lively, as can be seen from the programming of a single fortnight.[2] Balfour Gardiner had begun his concert series to promote the music of English composers. His concert of March 4th included works of Percy Grainger, Vaughan Williams, Arnold Bax, and J. B. McEwen. The most important work of the concert, according to *The Times*, was Holst's *The Cloud Messenger*. The following evening Donald Tovey presented one of his "Chelsea" concerts consisting of Beethoven's Piano Sonata, op. 54, Brahms's G minor Piano Quartet, op. 25, and Tovey's own *Air and Variations* for string quartet. On the 9th, Wood's Queen's Hall Orchestra played a mixed program of Beethoven, Strauss, Ponchielli, Saint-Saëns, Wagner, and Coleridge-Taylor; while on Monday, the 10th, the LSO played Smetana, Tchaikovsky, Vivaldi, Glazunov, and Wagner's *Rienzi* Overture. Also on the 10th, Beecham gave a performance of Delius's *Mass of Life*. March 12th saw Busoni playing an all-Chopin recital, and two nights later Beecham joined Josef Holbrooke in a program consisting almost entirely of the young composer's works, including excerpts from *Apollo and the Seaman*, the prelude to his opera *Dylan*, the tone poem *Ulalume*, and, as a finale, *Queen Mab*. On the afternoon of the 15th, Wood conducted a substantial program: Mozart's *Maurerische Trauermusik*, Bach's Violin Concerto in E, Beethoven's *Eroica*, the Mendelssohn Violin Concerto and Strauss's tone poem *Don Juan*. To close off the fortnight, Balfour Gardiner provided another program of English music, with Bantock's *Fifine at the Fair*, Bax's *In the Fairy Hills*, Delius's Piano Concerto in C minor, the première of Austin's E major Symphony, and Gardiner's own *Shepherd Fennel's Dance*.

This diversity of programming is reflected in the wide-ranging style of *The Planets*; and one must understand the kaleidoscopic nature of the London music scene in order to appreciate how well the composer has shaped it to his purpose. What has not been mentioned yet in this description of musical life in Edwardian London is the overwhelming presence of popular music. It must be dealt with in order to grasp fully Holst's accomplishment with *The Planets*, for the work was clearly a popular success, regardless of its rather short-lived critical acclaim.

Vaughan Williams told a story of a naval officer visiting

a lonely station on the Yorkshire coast inhabited only by a storekeeper and his wife. "You must be very lonely here," he said. "Yes, we depend a lot on our wireless." "What do you enjoy most on the wireless?" "Beethoven and Holst." [3]

This is not only a tribute to Holst's apparent standing at the height of his fame; it also sums up the whole of the rising middle class and its artistic tastes. While not specifically trained in music, the middle class could begin to relate to the more accessible of the classics, because their own popular idioms were nothing less than simple applications of the same language. Conversely, popular music became more sophisticated as composers became better trained. It is easy to smirk at the popular music of the time, especially as it is recalled in today's varieties and panto styles. But it must be remembered that the sources of the music were wide ranging and distinctions became blurred. The difference between the "shop ballad" (songs to be sung by amateurs at home) and Viennese light opera or Italian *opera buffa* was obscured by the well-crafted and singable tunes being written by otherwise "serious" composers such as Stanford (who was Holst's composition teacher at the RCM), Frederick Cowen, and Arthur Sullivan.[4] This crossing of styles – popular, folk, and light classical – allowed the middle class to indulge a vernacular propensity while developing their appreciation for the classics. Furthermore, much of the serious English music was, in terms of language, very close to a popular idiom, if more sophisticated in formal procedure.

Holst himself wrote and had published what he called "potboilers," an activity he regretted as time-wasting. Nevertheless, the *rhetorical* strategy remained with him; he continued occasionally to compose in what he dubbed a "lighter style," including such works as *Two Songs Without Words* (1906) and *Beni Mora* (1909–10).[5] These works were not potboilers, for they did not cater to popular taste; rather, they built upon it. Ultimately, this was to become a strategy in the writing of *The Planets*.

Holst in London – to 1914

When Holst first arrived in London he already thought of himself as a composer, having scored a success with an operetta entitled *Lansdown Castle, or the Sorcerer of Tewkesbury*. The music was judged to be somewhat in the style of Sullivan and more than one reviewer held up the work as evidence of great talent, and even genius. This appraisal by the provincial press was, at the very least, balanced by the difficulties of student life in London. Time spent at serious composition was equalled by time and energy spent making enough money to live. He worked as a trombonist in resort bands at Brighton and elsewhere; he wrote songs and partsongs – his potboilers – for extra money; he was organist at several churches. The variety of experience was enervating, but it set the pattern for his life until the success of *The Planets* earned him some breathing space. He managed to keep separate his different compositional styles, and he steadfastly pursued serious music as his ultimate goal.

In 1907, already carrying a full load between the James Allen School and St.

Paul's Girls' School, Holst took a position at Morley College for Working Men and Women. During this period, Holst submitted a large work, *Sita*, for the Ricordi Opera Prize. He had great faith in it, but it did not win the cash prize. According to Imogen Holst, his disappointment was great, not only because he was convinced of its merit, but because he really needed the money.

To help him over this time, Vaughan Williams offered him a monetary gift to allow him to take a holiday. Holst accepted and chose Algeria as his destination. Algeria would change his outlook forever. His interest in Hindu philosophy and oriental subjects in general had been primarily intellectual in nature. Africa brought that world to life in a way which moved him greatly. "I am quite at home here now," he wrote to his wife, Isobel, describing his visits to various churches and mosques, "but the chief glory of Algiers is the native quarter . . . with [its] dirty shops or houses and the 'smell of the East'!" He was taken with the Arabs, whom he considered aristocratic, but equally so with the "wild, dirty-looking blackguards with the faces of fiends." As his daughter described it, life there was

full of unexpected happenings. His return ticket was stolen by a native. He helped to rescue an English woman who had been deserted by her French husband. He listened to an Arab musician playing the same short phrase on his flute for hour after hour.[6]

Life was to change for him after this; not so much externally, for his need for money would plague him for some time to come, but internally, spiritually. He began composing in order to express his understanding of the world. This attitude led to a number of real successes, particularly his four sets of *Choral Hymns from the Rig Veda*, and his folksong-based *A Somerset Rhapsody*. His school-teaching efforts were also paying off, with his groups giving perform-ances of increasingly higher quality. In 1910–11, he spearheaded a revival of Purcell's *The Fairy Queen*. He was also getting better performances of his own works through the sponsorship of Balfour Gardiner who began programming Holst's music in his orchestral series. *Beni Mora*, subtitled *An Oriental Suite*, was performed in 1912 to mixed reviews.[7] A few months later Gardiner programmed *The Phantastes Suite*. Holst was to withdraw the work after this performance, but it received good reviews, particularly for the composer's ability as an orchestrator. Francis Toye, writing in *The Bystander*, called Holst the English Stravinsky, claiming to discern more logic in his music than in the Russian master.[8]

Actually, Holst's music seems to have had quite a bit of exposure during these years (1908–14; see Appendix 1, Table 1). During this seven-year span he had at least fifty-three separate performances of his works, the peak years being 1911, 1912, and 1913, with eleven, eleven, and fifteen concerts respectively. When his school events are added, and the inclusion of songs in solo recitals considered, the totals are somewhat higher. Among orchestral works, *A Somerset Rhapsody*, with ten performances, was the most often heard work, though *Beni Mora*, appearing only in the last three years, had six performances. Holst's choral music received more attention. For example, the *Choral Hymns from the Rig Veda*, counting all four sets, were programmed at least fourteen times during the seven-year span. These numbers suggest that Holst had become something of a "known quantity," and he had quite a few published editions as well. In particular, his choral music had become established, having received numerous performances throughout England.

These successes, however, did not wholly satisfy the composer. When Clifford Bax remembered Holst during these years as "an apparent failure," it is likely that he was reflecting his friend's self-appraisal.[9] Holst, nearing forty years of age, had not succeeded in making a livelihood out of composing. He was forced to continue in his role of schoolmaster, a career which gave him satisfaction but which still was inferior in the minds of most people. In Germany his music was considered too close to English populist style to be effective in that country. Letters around this time to his closest friend, Vaughan Williams, expressed frustration and confusion. He saw in himself a lack of background and no clear guidance into the future.[10] Much of his success outside London was due to the influence of friends such as W. G. Whittaker, who championed Holst's choral music through his chorus work in Newcastle; and Dan Godfrey, a fellow RCM student whose Winter Gardens orchestra in Bournemouth performed a variety of his works. Holst's most recent large work of this time, *The Cloud Messenger* (1913), had been performed at a Balfour Gardiner concert without the acclaim he had received for the withdrawn *Phantastes Suite*.

It would have been immediately after the evening of the performance of *The Cloud Messenger* that he wrote to Frank Duckworth, who was preparing his Blackburn choir for a March 10th program featuring Holst's music: "The 'Cloud' did not go well and the whole thing has been a blow to me. I'm 'fed up' with music, especially my own." Furthermore, one of the composer's main hopes for further success was apparently about to disappear. It was Gardiner who had been responsible for much of Holst's exposure in London, through his "English" concerts, but there was some doubt as to his continuing them. Gardiner, perhaps by way of consolation and encouragement, invited Holst to accompany him and Arnold and Clifford Bax on a trip through Spain and Mallorca. He accepted the invitation, and Bax's account of that trip suggests that Holst was truly melancholy. The success of Duckworth's concert was apparently not enough to pull the composer out of his depression.[11] He avoided conversation as a rule, and often he would strike out on his own while the others roamed about as a group.

During this trip, however, Clifford and Holst discovered a mutual interest in astrology, setting the stage for *The Planets*. In the summer of 1914, Holst moved his family out of London to Thaxted, and between his quiet garden there and his new soundproof room at St. Paul's he began sketching out his suite for large orchestra.

London after the war

In England, the music scene was changing, but not as fast as in other European countries. Composers were nationalistic rather than international in their concerns, introspective rather than cosmopolitan in their outlook. Examples include Vaughan Williams's (revised) "London" Symphony, *The Lark Ascending*, *Hugh the Drover*, and "Pastoral" Symphony; and Arthur Bax's *November Woods*, the *Symphonic Variations*, and *Tintagel*. In comparison with the works of Stravinsky and Schoenberg, not to mention the experiments of the younger French composers, British music seemed quaint and isolated in its nostalgic mood. Even a work as strong and "European" as Elgar's Cello Concerto (1919) belonged to an earlier stylistic phase compared with Schoenberg's *Pierrot Lunaire*.

This seemingly populist trend sets a context for *The Planets*, as Holst was to use folk and other populist elements as major characterizations in many of the movements. At the same time the function of such elements, both within local textures and larger formal concerns, is much different from what had become standard English usage, approaching Mahler's ideas of stylistic tension and metaphor.[12] Furthermore, Mahler's use of tunes from non-symphonic (and therefore seemingly inferior) styles is echoed in *The Planets*; yet Holst's usage would not have carried the *angst* felt in the Austrian composer's music. This last is due to the greater sense of objectivity in Holst (Mahler made autobiographical allusions clear in his works, while Holst maintained an emotional distance from his); but perhaps more significant is the musical environment in which *The Planets* was launched. As is clear from any social history of music in both Edwardian and post-war London, popular music became a strong cultural force, and "legitimate" musical efforts such as the folkloric and nationalistic movements can be seen as responses to the growing social significance of the various popular styles. As was mentioned at the beginning of this chapter, Holst felt an affinity with this "vulgar" world. There are a number of comments made by the composer, particularly with reference to Hammersmith, where he lived for many years. Therefore, the vulgar element in *The Planets* must be considered qualitatively different from Mahler's melancholic and introspective usage. Holst's popular references, like the "topics" found in eighteenth-century music, brought the music to the people.

While the music of British composers during these years may be seen as a response to the prevailing cultural trends at home, it must also be viewed as part of a musico-political dialogue with current continental trends. Reviews written at the time suggest that critics approached their work in this manner, and arguments as to the validity of one school of composition over another were often heated. The musical debate was underpinned by a much larger philosophical discussion concerning the rational and the irrational. On a popular level these issues surfaced as a renewed interest in astrology, spiritualism, and other pseudo-disciplines which dealt with areas of life that science could not address. These issues may not have been dealt with in popular music which concentrated on domestic comedy, romance, and various social topics; yet Holst's use of popular idiom in *The Planets* represented a special kind of novelty which both brought serious psychological and spiritual ideas into general musical parlance and elevated the *popular* to a more serious artistic level.

It was in this climate that Holst's suite was introduced, and if popularity could not have been legitimately forecast, a sympathetic and interested hearing certainly could.

Holst's reputation through the war years and after

In 1911 Holst had decided to do whatever was necessary to get his music performed. After Balfour Gardiner discontinued his concert series, however, it became much more difficult to get his work programmed. His choral music had a strong following in parts of England, but his orchestral works were getting very little exposure. Furthermore, his work on *The Planets* kept him from attempting any other large orchestral piece, and school activities continued to monopolize his schedule. During the war this situation continued. (See Appendix 1, Table 2.)

Holst had completed *The Planets* in 1916 and, before leaving for Salonika, he was given a private performance of it as a gift from Balfour Gardiner. The unofficial première of the work (without *Venus* or *Neptune*) took place at a

15

Royal Philharmonic Society Concert in February 1919, with Adrian Boult conducting, while the composer was still away. It is interesting that, while it received generally good notices, it seemed not to create a real stir.

Holst's most important breakthrough was the triumph of *The Hymn of Jesus* early in 1920, just a few months before the first full performance of *The Planets*. The work is based on a text from the Apocryphal Gospels. The public's interest in spiritualism and oriental mysticism might well have predisposed them favorably, but *The Hymn of Jesus* was no mere fashionable entertainment. Tovey called it "the thing in itself"; an experience so immediate and thoroughly real that it transcended mere music-making.[13] It also offered the public its first glimpse of Holst's "alternative" theory: his use of colorful mediant chords (chords whose roots are three scale degrees higher or lower than the tonic) rather than the standard tonal progressions; his use of chords as blocks of sound; and his emphasis on musical character. While a general audience might not be able to discuss "theory" or make its way through musical "logic," there seems to have been no trouble in being moved by the character of the music.

Holst was consistent in his application of harmonic principles, but his system was not based on nineteenth-century ideas of consistent sonority. Pure triads are contrasted with polychords and unisons in response to both the sense of the text and the musical development. Yet his musical principles were so novel for the audience that the system came across only as an intuited experience. There was no set of particulars to be addressed by traditional analysis. Hence the music was heard as going beyond mere representation of mysticism, to the "mystical" itself, thus establishing Holst, himself, as a mystic.

The Hymn of Jesus was a true success. One person involved in the first performances has written that to those who were young then,

and eager for something that would lift us out of the rut of common experience, this very new music, which for all its novelty of expression seemed firmly rooted in the great tradition of English choral writing, came first as a shock, then as a revelation. . . . [I]t seemed [to be] a vindication of the right of the English composer to be considered as a potential contributor to the general musical culture of the world at large.[14]

It is here, then, that the public Holst begins, as both mystic and progressive composer. By the time *The Planets* was given its first full performance eight months later, the London audience was primed for a major event. These two works comprised the majority of offerings from Holst's output over the next few years. However, there was a renewed interest in all of Holst's earlier works as well. The Holst Press Cuttings Collection has programs or reviews for twenty-four major performances of various pieces in 1921 – twice the number from 1920. *The Hymn of Jesus* and *The Planets* both were programmed as fast as they could be learned. In 1922 Holst collected reviews for another thirty-three major performances.

It is ironic that by the time *The Planets* became successful, it was, for Holst, *passé*. His maturing technique allowed him to develop better ways of dealing with formal issues and more intense means of establishing musical character. Rather than continue with the specific language of the suite, he chose – as did Stravinsky at about the same time – to pursue what must have seemed more interesting and challenging issues. Nevertheless, his audience continued to look to *The Planets* as a model for his new works. As a result, the greater subtlety and detachment of such works as his *Choral Symphony* (1923–4), *Egdon Heath* (1927), and the *Double Concerto* (1929) were misunderstood by the general audience. Even a work as apparently delightful as *A Fugal Concerto* (1923) was slighted by reviewers, who called it desiccated and without warmth. In this specific case, as with the negative reviews of most of Holst's later major compositions, there is reference back to earlier, easier works.[15] In another telling situation, *Egdon Heath* was decried in *The Times* while, on the same page, Holst – as the composer of *The Planets* – is held up as the standard against which other composers must be measured. In a very real sense, the success of this composition plagued him for the rest of his life. As an event, it was like a great stellar convergence: public interest and need happened to coincide with what Holst had to offer. While he was to produce a number of truly great musical works over the last fourteen years of his life, he was never able, nor ever willing, to achieve the pinnacle of popular success again.

17

2

Genesis

It is difficult to establish the point at which Holst began in earnest to consider a large suite based on astrological influences. There are no early sketches or studies for such a suite; and, in fact, the piece seems to have sprung virtually full grown out of his head during the summer vacation of 1914. There is mention of the sketch for *Mars* having been completed during the summer of 1914, soon after the composer had moved out of London to Thaxted, but when he began it is unknown. Clifford Bax quotes Holst as saying that he had had the intention of composing the work for two years, during which time "it seemed of itself more and more definitely to be taking form."[1] There is no way of knowing whether this referred to the period of composition (1914–16) or to the period before his first sketches. The latter possibility seems to be ruled out by Bax's earlier belief that Holst had not known much about astrology before their 1913 holiday. On the other hand, neither Bax's claim nor Holst's reminiscence can be taken absolutely on faith, for neither was meant as an attempt to fix the precise date of the work's inception.

Another possibility, as Michael Short suggests, is that Holst had begun considering a suite for large orchestra in 1912, after hearing Schoenberg's *Five Pieces for Orchestra*.[2] That suite had been given a second performance in January of 1914, and, with the added impetus of Holst's growing interest in astrology, his ideas which had been incubating in the abstract for nearly two years may have been brought to life. Given the suite's working title – *Seven Pieces for Large Orchestra* – this is an attractive scenario. Holst would have presumably been thinking of an abstract work similar to Schoenberg's, in which he could give free rein to his growing orchestral imagination. This was not his typical approach to composition; he was almost always influenced by some extra-musical idea. So it is possible that this scheme lay dormant until the astrological theme presented itself to him.

Such a hypothesis is borne out musically in the fact that it is the orchestration which gives the piece its immediate communicative power. The musical surface is never very complex from a theoretical point of view; and sometimes

18

(as in *Mercury*) the simplest musical idea is richly transformed by his creative orchestral technique. In a piano reduction, the scales and arpeggios in this movement are rather aimless and dull. It is the overlapping of instrumental entries and the quick movement of a figure across the orchestral terrain that imbue the music with character and excitement. Furthermore, *Neptune*, as the musical and metaphorical culmination of the suite, is also the high point of its creative orchestration. And, finally, this apex appears less influenced by Stravinsky's eccentric and piquant orchestral palette and more by the mesmeric and hazy *Klangfarben* style of the third movement of Schoenberg's *Five Pieces for Orchestra*.[3]

Since it is unclear at what point Holst had arrived at a working concept, there is no way of ascertaining when he first began his efforts on the piece by sketching *Mars*. The composer is on record as saying the movement was completed before the outbreak of the war, i.e. before August 1914. He contended that the piece was not a depiction of the war, though this may have been meant as a denial of narrative programmaticism, i.e. he was not following the model supplied by Strauss's *Ein Heldenleben*. Yet everyone in England was aware of the growing hostilities on the Continent, and the outbreak of war had been anticipated for months before the formal declarations. Holst had written his *Dirge for Two Veterans* in the spring of 1914, and it is difficult not to assume some personal preoccupation with the theme. There are at least two earlier works of his which also deal with war and tragedy: *Battle Hymn* from the first set of *Choral Hymns from the Rig Veda* is an obvious example; and *A Somerset Rhapsody* (1906–7), Holst's most successful folksong work, weaves a psychological tale of lost love and military bravado which ends in tragedy. So Holst might well have been following his own predilection, brought into focus by the rising hostilities in Europe, when he chose to begin his efforts with "The Bringer of War."

In any case, to begin with the planet Mars was unusual, in astrological terms, because Mercury is the first planet (after the Sun and the Moon) listed in the manuals. Holst did, in fact, list *Mercury* as "no. 1" in one notebook, thereby raising the distinct possibility that his first idea was simply to collect the *Planets* in the obvious order. However, opening with the more disturbing character of *Mars* allows a more dramatic and compelling working out of the musical material. Each *Planet* provides a further metamorphosis of the gestures and metaphors of *Mars* in a psychological plot suggesting the desirability of the mystical state over life in the physical world (see Chapter 6).

These issues show up in Holst's letters to Vaughan Williams, when he speaks of the Hindu philosophy of life and death and the doctrine of Dharma.[4] But they are also written across almost every page of his Sanskrit works – the symphonic poem *Indra* (1903), the operas *Sita* (1906) and *Savitri* (1908), and the various sets of *Choral Hymns from the Rig Veda* (1908–12). Just as interesting is the *Dirge and Hymeneal* of 1915. The text of this work focuses on the contrast between death and the joy of life, all cast within a single musical characterization, stoic and dutiful, with a buoyancy held gently in check by an overall serenity. That this small choral piece should have been the model for *Saturn* is of crucial significance for an understanding of *The Planets* as a whole. It points up the central paradox: the overtly physical *Mars* as both life and death against *Neptune, the Mystic*, seeking life where the physical world senses an end to life.

Apart from *Mars* and *Mercury*, Holst followed the normal astrological scheme; at the same time, he ordered the movements around opposing poles, projecting an outward journey through the solar system and a parallel, psychological plot. To do this he had to take some license with the astrological characters (see Chapter 4). It may be that he had always expected to "abuse" astrology just a bit, for he had not originally included the planets' names as movement titles. On the final manuscript Holst squeezed in the names around the movement numbers and subtitles, perhaps at the time he decided to give the suite its official name. The title page of the manuscript was not changed, and it reads simply *"Seven Pieces for Large Orchestra."*[5]

With a psychological program in place and a musical plot to hold the movements together as a whole, the work can be seen as following Beethoven's *Pastoral* Symphony and Berlioz's *Symphonie Fantastique*, as well as the symphonies of Mahler. The stumbling block for Holst's commentators, with regard to this comparison, is that the composer did not subject his material to an accepted symphonic treatment. It has been pointed out in every discussion of Holst's compositional technique that he did not make use of classic developmental procedure. His use of the word "suite" with reference to *The Planets*, implying a non-symphonic approach, has been used to support the contention that he was unable to come to terms with the demands of large-scale forms. Yet his structures and formal principles are derived from classic models, and there is a clear sense of development in the suite, albeit in a distinctly modern form (Chapter 4).

Origins and models

The basis for the misunderstanding lay in Holst's thoughts on form. As mentioned earlier, his point of view was laid out in "The mystic, the philistine and the artist," distinguishing between technique and a preoccupation with mechanics on the one hand, and artistic vision on the other: "I read the other day that 'music is waiting for the master who will combine the counterpoint of Palestrina, the form of Mozart, the melody of Schubert, and the instrumentation of Beethoven'. He might be a master joiner, but certainly not an Artist." In this spirit, his own works always develop along individual lines. Holst did recognize the influence of Wagner in his early compositions; works which, true to form, he saw as mainly uninspired. On the other hand, he continually sought to allow the musical material of each composition to inspire his formal principles and large-scale structure. So, in looking for precedents for *The Planets*, the analyst who tries to fit Holst's schemes into prior models goes against one of the basic principles of the composer's working method. On the other hand, there are certain structural features which demonstrate the interaction between accepted formal conventions and the requirements of the various movements of the suite.

The dramatic use of recapitulation which characterizes many nineteenth-century sonata forms is an essential part of Holst's formal syntax. Among his works that predate *The Planets*, *A Somerset Rhapsody* (1906–7) stands out as an example of this. The program of the work, based on the original texts of its folksong themes, deals with the loss of a lover. To project this, Holst returns his lovers' theme in the key of B♭ minor, a tritone away from the home key of E minor; and his apparent return to E minor is so overlaid with chromaticism as to bring about a loss, for the listener, of the sense of arrival home.[6]

In looking at formal procedures in *The Planets*, we find that a similar working method obtains. In *Mars*, a large three-part structure unfolds. While the scheme is not a strict sonata form, it does use the principle of tension among keys to be reconciled in the reprise.

	Exposition		Contrast		Recapitulation		Coda
	Th 1	Th 2	Th 3	Th 2	Th 1	Th 2	
Measure:	1	29	66	96	110	148	167
Pedal:	g	c	–	b	g	g	c
Key:	?	?	various	?(c)	c	c	c

The principal innovation is one of tonal function: rather than establish a clear functional context at the outset, Holst avoids it. By allowing his material – which is formally quite simple – to be construed ambiguously, the composer creates the tension needed to propel the movement forward without resorting to conventional grammar. When traditional grammatical devices do occur – root motion down by a perfect 5th or diatonic sequencing – they are frustrated at the point of arrival. The opening is sufficiently stabilized by the long pedal tones so as to be perceived as exposition rather than development; but it is only at the point of the reprise (m. 110) that the opening material is made to "make sense": the opening theme is set up to be heard as a V chord in the home key of C minor. This establishes a sense of recapitulation, but the pounding clash between C and D♭ major chords at the end shows the form in service to high drama.

Jupiter makes similar use of the sonata principle. The introduction establishes the home key of C major, but the first theme is presented in D major, thus using the exposition to set up the essential harmonic tension. The second theme is in the dominant, G. The famous center theme (known to anyone who grew up in England in the 1920s and 1930s by the words "I Vow to Thee, My Country") takes the place of a development section (m. 194 ff); however, the tune is driven by the principle of developing variation and is built from a motive tying all of the themes of *Jupiter* together. The reprise establishes both the first and second themes in the home key.

	Exposition			Development			Recapitulation			??	Coda
	Intro	Th 1	Th 2	Trans	Chor	Trans	Th 1	Th 2		Chor	
Measure:	1	65	108	156	194	234	305	348	356	388	395
Key:	C	D	G	x	E♭	x	C	(D♭)	C	g♯	C

There are formal problems with the keys of E♭ and G♯ minor as well as with the unexpected interpolation of the center theme in a *Klangfarben* texture at the end. But these anomalies can be accounted for within the larger context of the suite. E♭ was the framing key for *Venus* in which the C minor key of *Mars* is transformed into a major key via an E♭ chord with added 6th (E♭–G–B♭–C being an extension of C–E♭–G). The key of G♯ minor with the *Klangfarben* texture is used as a portent of *Neptune* which begins with a focus on that key.

This use of composite form to create a single work out of several movements is also based on a prior model established, as mentioned earlier, by such compositions as the *Symphonie Fantastique*. Holst had used this idea in *Beni Mora* (1909–10) when he brought thematic work from the first two movements into the finale. In *The Planets*, the composer achieves a gradual accumulation of motivic and theoretical relationships. The use of ostinatos, oscillating 2nds, false cadences and the like, accrues through each successive movement, intensifying their effect. At the same time, motives are followed by their own variants, which themselves are manipulated by harmonic and rhythmic tension into transformed characterizations. An example is the oscillating major

2nd at the end of *Venus*, a placid and serene gesture established in a stable tonal area. It can be traced to the plunging 2nds of *Mars* (mm. 29–34, 62–4, 133–6, 167–72); then it reappears as the cold and unstable "ticking" 2nds which open *Saturn*. By the end of this latter movement, the activity is once again serene, and it contributes to the stoic nature of *Neptune* when it returns in various guises, but most clearly in the oscillation of the final two chords. In fact, as will be seen in Chapter 5, the final section of *Neptune* is a summing up of most of the theoretical issues brought up in previous movements.

While the technical parallel exists between Holst's suite and Berlioz's symphony, the narrative programmaticism of the latter was obviously not intended for the former. In this regard, Debussy's *Nocturnes* is a more likely model. Holst probably heard a number of the latter's works when they were performed in London in 1909, and, while he professed little liking for the music, there is enough similarity between certain works of the two composers, in the concepts of orchestration and motivic display, to suggest a more than passing interest for Holst in what Debussy was doing. Principally, there is the notion of musical character apart from the narrative programmaticism of Berlioz and Richard Strauss. In fact, Holst's music gains greatly when viewed in this light. Virtually all of his instrumental works come to life, as formal entities, when the musical material is heard as projecting metaphors of character and human action. The psychological program behind each movement of *The Planets* is activated by the same metaphoric action as found in a work such as *Nocturnes*, for the two composers appear to work from the same rhetorical principles. Debussy based his work on the French Symbolist movement which was heavily influenced by the techniques of musical character practised by Wagner. And it is through Wagner, as common ancestor, that Holst's debt to the composer of the *Nocturnes* can be understood.

Finally, there is the possibility that Holst was building on the programmatic/symphonic concept of his friend, Ralph Vaughan Williams. It is interesting that the oscillating 2nd at the end of *Venus* can also be found, using the same pitches and key (B♭ and C in E♭ major), in Vaughan Williams's *Sea Symphony* which predates *Venus* by a number of years. In the closing moments of the symphony's finale (*The Explorers*) this oscillation, stemming from the opening of the movement, is heard within the key of E♭; at which point a pedal tone on G shifts the tonal emphasis toward C minor, and the sense of serenity is lost in the haunted nature of the explorer and the lurking menace of the unknowable sea. There are obvious differences between the two works, but the idea of using a series of symphonic-length movements in the service of a psychological program might stem from this source. The possibility of a symphonic concept was recognized by a number of early reviewers when they discussed *Mercury* and *Uranus* as scherzo movements and *Venus* as "the slow movement of a symphony."[7] Likewise, several of the "excerpt" performances grouped the movements in such a symphonic arrangement. The following are good examples: *Mars, Venus, Mercury,* and *Jupiter*; or *Mars, Saturn, Uranus,* and *Jupiter*. The idea of a double symphony is also found in early discussions of the work. In this perspective, *Jupiter* serves as the finale of the first symphony and the opening of the second. Its use of "real tunes," as reviewers sometimes called them, and its reference to sonata form allow it to work well in this double capacity.

Of course, not all of the movements of the suite work within the sonata principle, nor is there an absolute need to hear the work as a whole in order for individual movements to make sense. What is important to note is that Holst, as part of his rhetorical method, was able to balance purely musical needs with the requirements of communication. This was, perhaps, an unconscious choice; nevertheless, it reflects his double world of composer and teacher, visionary and communicator. And the immediate result was the possibility of acceptance in the two Londons – the academic and the popular.

Specific influences of the outside world or of other composers' work are few outside those already mentioned. Reviewers – with a greater sense of authority than was warranted – often cited parallels, particularly between *Uranus* and Dukas' *L'Apprenti Sorcier*, and between *Mars* and *Ein Heldenleben*. These are comparisons of character rather than of technique.[8] With regard to orchestration, the work calls for a large and varied ensemble, but this was a general trend up until the war. Furthermore, Holst seldom calls for an orchestral *tutti*, instead using the orchestra more in the manner of Debussy. That being said, it must be clarified that *The Planets* does not use Debussy's orchestra (if such a thing can be said to have existed), nor his particular instrumental combinations – these are Holst's own. Colin Matthews, in his preface to the new edition of the score, mentions the possibility of Holst following Strauss in using the bass oboe, and that the tenor tuba might have been suggested by Stravinsky's use of it. However, Holst's use of these instruments suggests a clear purpose for them as parts of the whole; there is no sense of their being added for their own sakes. The use of female chorus may well have been suggested by Debussy's *Sirènes* (from *Nocturnes*); yet, as Michael Short has pointed out, it was a natural choice for someone teaching in a girls' school. Beyond this, Holst would have been searching for a sound to match the mystic's unimaginable vision. A mixed chorus would have been too close to

Table 2.1 Orchestral forces used in *The Planets*

Woodwinds	Pitched Percussion
4 flutes	bells
(2 doubling piccolos;	glockenspiel
1 doubling bass flute)	xylophone
3 B♭ or A clarinets	celesta
1 bass clarinet	timpani (2 players)
3 oboes (1 doubling bass oboe)	
1 english horn	Unpitched Percussion
3 bassoons	cymbals
1 double bassoon	gong
	side drum
Brass	bass drum
6 french horns	
4 trumpets	Strings
3 trombones	2 harps
1 tenor tuba	organ
1 bass tuba	6-part female chorus

the conventional cathedral chorus, but the sound of soprano choir coming out of the dense *Klangfarben* texture proved to be just right.

Up to this time Holst had been developing a colorful orchestra, but not an exceptionally large one. For *The Planets*, however, his concept required much larger forces. (See Table 2.1.)

If the model here is the orchestra of Richard Strauss, this is not specifically a matter of size. Strauss's principles of orchestration included the concept of balanced instrumental choirs, both to allow full doubling in complex textures and to restate the full texture of a passage in different homogeneous instrumentation. Both functions appear in *The Planets*.

For example, *Mars* uses a large chordal texture which calls for extensive doubling with choirs of equal size. Sections of themes 1 and 2 (mm. 21–42 and 43–66) consist of a gradual piling up of instruments doubling the parallel chord movement which constitutes the themes. Holst uses only the number of instruments in each choir necessary to cover the chord structures; the structures themselves require the large forces. Another case, involving less volume, is in *Venus*, mm. 11–19, where the lush chords of the harps are doubled quietly, but completely, in the woodwinds and french horns. In the first presentation of the center theme of *Jupiter*, mm. 193–205, the melody is done as a unison doubling between french horns and strings, with flutes, bassoons, and harps doubling on the accompanying chords.

Chordal textures are thematic in many of the movements, and Holst often used homogeneous choirs by themselves to cover such passages, so that the texture could be heard in a single color. This follows the second reason for using the Straussian balanced choir concept. The opening passage of *Venus*, for example, features the four flutes in descending chords while a contrasting color is heard in the ascending oboe triads (mm. 3–5). The flute choir returns in *Saturn* for the dirge-like middle theme (mm. 53–66), which the composer referred to as his "four-flute theme." In *Neptune*, the shifting harmonies beginning at m. 22 are scored variously for trumpets and trombones; oboes, english horn, and bass oboe; bassoon choir and french horns; and finally for full brass with low register double reeds.

Another use for extended winds, more practical than aesthetic, is found in *Mercury*, where the bi-tonal scales are partitioned along tonal lines and assigned to instrumental partners: flute I and II; oboe I and II; bassoon, english horn, and oboe. This helps to keep things in tune, as no single group has to negotiate the tritone relationship between keys. It also is a practical consideration of the issues of breathing and concentration particular to woodwinds. It is therefore clear that Holst's use of exotic instruments and large forces was not really self-indulgent; the compositional design and concept required this large orchestra.

Perhaps the clearest borrowing is one of musical character: the center theme of *Jupiter* comes very close to the *Nimrod* variation in Elgar's *Enigma Variations*. Holst paid special tribute to this piece as signalling for him the beginning of the renaissance of English music. Besides the fact that both themes are written in chorale style, they both project a sense of yearning upward toward greater fulfillment. In *Nimrod* this is done through a build up of texture and instrumentation, the gradual upward contour of the melody, and the reiteration of gestures just before the reprise of the opening phrase. In *Jupiter*, the sense of yearning is created through the upward spiral of the melody which never ends. The tune finishes on the dominant and begins again, without the listener knowing quite how it happened, at the next higher octave. *Jupiter* was characterized in the reviews as the most English of the *Planets*, and its center theme may have been a thinly veiled portrayal of Elgar as the leader of the revival of an English school of composition.

Chronology and working method

Holst's working method seems to have been to carry on a double life: school work and small compositional projects were done during the week and work

Table 2.2 Chronology of Holst's works, 1914–16

Dirge for Two Veterans	by 27 June 1914
Mars	before August 1914
Vigil of Pentecost	before autumn 1914
Venus	autumn 1914
Jupiter	late 1914
Nunc Dimittis	by 4 April 1915
Dirge and Hymeneal	immediately before Saturn, 1915
Saturn	summer 1915
Uranus	by August 1915
Neptune	autumn 1915
Japanese Suite	late 1915
Mercury	early 1916
(suite orchestration completed during 1917)	

on *The Planets* was saved for weekends and the summer vacation. The best chronology we have for this period shows a mixture of small works interspersed with the writing of the individual movements (see Table 2.2).

Sometimes, as was mentioned with reference to *Dirge and Hymeneal* and *Saturn*, these smaller pieces served as technical or character studies for the specific *Planet* at hand. For instance, the opening of *A Vigil of Pentecost* uses the contrary chordal counterpoint of *Venus*; *The Dance of the Marionettes* from the *Japanese Suite* shares significant characteristics with the trio of *Mercury*. But in all cases the relationship concerns musical figures rather than large-scale formal patterns or musical dialect. None of these smaller pieces could be construed as a sketch for the *Planet* it seems to have influenced; rather, the similarity of material and the reuse of motives point to Holst's general preoccupation with particular musical ideas during this time. This seems to have been especially the case with the *Dirge* which carries not only musical material but character associations which were to be important for *Saturn*.

The constant overlap of his two lives seems to have led to a terrible stress on the composer which was only partly alleviated by his sound-proof room at St. Paul's and his hilltop cottage in Thaxted. Both of these conveniences point to Holst's growing need for isolation – from wage-earning and from the stimulus of the outside world. The new facilities at the school seem to have been of special importance. He is known to have spoken of the spell which the room had over him, and his daughter recounts in her biography the Sunday picnics that the two of them had in his room at St. Paul's while he was doing weekend composing. In spite of his need for tranquillity when composing, his daily work brought him into contact with many conflicting ideas and music. Michael Short maintains that Holst would retreat to his sound-proof room at the end of a day to set down the various musical thoughts which had come to him during his work. The routine seems not to have produced a sketch book filled with things for the suite in progress, yet the amalgamation of formal processes and musical dialects found in the work suggests that his "outer" life had some influence on his "inner" life as he developed his first large-scale instrumental work. And the fact that the rollicking, good-natured fun of *Uranus* gives way to the distant and isolated style of *Neptune* demonstrates where the composer's preferences lay.

Holst's primary concern throughout the months of composing necessary to put the suite together would have been to hold on to the central idea. Working one day a week on the suite with so much else to do would make so highly integrated a score virtually impossible. Sketching out one movement at a time and in sequence might have allowed the composer to keep track of his developing ideas. By refraining from step-by-step development patterns, he also made it possible for motivic variations to build up from movement to movement without needing to explain them in any conscious musical way. The exception which suggests the rule is *Mercury* which was composed out of sequence, and which also has the weakest relationship to other movements.

During his sketch period, Holst worked on piano scores which he would have students and colleagues play through with him. The scores were marked with instrumentation, and gradually each movement was transferred to full score. Much of the final manuscript was not written by the composer himself, indicating how much he was indebted to his colleagues (particularly Nora Day and Valley Lasker) in preparing the score. This was certainly a practical matter, for besides lacking the time to do all the work on schedule, Holst suffered from chronic neuritis in his writing hand, making it often impossible for him to copy for any period of length.

In September of 1918, already having begun work on *The Hymn of Jesus*, Holst received the gift of a performance of his suite from his old friend, Balfour Gardiner. It had been a time of waiting for the composer. He had applied for an appointment with the YMCA as a music organizer in war internment camps on the Continent. After changing his name from von Holst to Holst (on advice from the YMCA who thought his name too German for effective war work) he received an assignment and was waiting to hear when he would be shipped out. With the prospect of a run-through of his composition, the strain of uncertainty was replaced with excitement and purpose, and Holst put his friends and pupils to work preparing a full set of parts for the performance. The choir of St. Paul's Girls' School was trained as the chorus for *Neptune*, and on the 29th of September, after an hour of rehearsal, the first performance of *The Planets* took place.

There were several public performances of incomplete versions of the suite while Holst was in Salonika with the YMCA, and when he returned more performances were scheduled with Holst himself conducting. But the event of note for the composer at this time was the première of *The Hymn of Jesus* in March 1920. This was to create a sensation, setting the stage for the reception of the first full public performance of *The Planets* on the 15th of November that year. With the success of his choral work and with plans in place for his opera *The Perfect Fool* underway, he may have anticipated the première of his suite with a sense of anticlimax. To be sure, Holst seems to have responded with unexpected reluctance to the acclaim which greeted his work. Accounts of his being called on to acknowledge applause after performances of his works describe him as seeming embarrassed and ill-at-ease. His difficulty with journalists is also documented. His daughter described him as "the despair of photographers and press reporters" for whom he was fidgety and unhelpful, often scowling while maintaining a glum silence.[9] On the other hand, as Short has pointed out, Holst saw the fickleness of a general public more interested in novelty than in art, and totally unsuited to follow his musical vision to the next stage.

3

Reception

It is hard today to imagine the impact of the language of *The Planets* on its
original audience. While a good deal of Europe's avant-garde music was being
gradually introduced in London, British taste was still polarized between the
nineteenth-century classics on the one hand, and simple entertainment styles
on the other. Part of the success of the suite must be attributed to the variety
of language from one movement to the next. Yet a study of the reviews of
various performances suggests that it was not until the suite was heard in its
entirety that it was so widely acclaimed. Also to be considered is the reception
of *The Hymn of Jesus*, which was certainly as enthusiastic and as wide ranging
as that of the suite. Perhaps the most important point is that, unlike most
compositions, *The Planets* was introduced over a two-year period, and by 1920
many of the movements were "like old friends," as claimed by L. Dunton
Green in the *Arts Gazette* (29 November 1919). This reviewer was clearly on
Holst's side, and early on had written about how disturbed he was that the
suite was not being played in its complete form. "It was an injustice to the
composer to rob his planetary system of the two stars whose soft light would
have relieved the fierce glare of the five others" (*Arts Gazette*, 8 March 1919).
During his life, Holst had developed friendships with a number of critics, for
example Edwin Evans and Richard Capell, and had been championed
professionally by others, including Donald Tovey, Francis Toye, and Ernest
Newman. There were others, mostly writing anonymously, who did not like
the composer or who found his early Sanskrit works more to their liking.[1]
   Among serious music lovers two points of view existed, very well described
by H. C. Colles in *The Times* (8 March 1919) in an exhortation to adventurous
listening:

There are at present two clearly defined lines of thought in composition, exampled by
two works lately heard for the first time in London: Stanford's String Quartet . . . and
Holst's orchestral suite, *The Planets*. The one holds that the listener should be as far
as possible relieved from the distractions of this particular form of discrimination; that
it is the composer's business to make himself intelligible by talking in a familiar and

polished style of speech; the other that, the composer saying what he likes as he likes, it is for the listener to make sense of it as he can. Neither can get away from the fact that, whether the composer helps him or not, the listener has got to make sense of it; and it is only when he has done so that his real joy in the music can begin. . . . The artist takes [risks] – indeed plunges more recklessly through them with each effort – why should not [the listener] take them too? He has only to look beyond the bogeys both of his own limitations and those of the composer for his adventures of the spirit to begin.

The review of the Birmingham performance of 10 October 1920 (comprising *Mars, Venus, Mercury, Saturn,* and *Jupiter*) in the *Manchester Guardian* (11 October 1920) forms something of a rebuttal to this plea.

The intellectualization of his musical ideas constitutes the difficulty of his music to the normal ear. From thinking in beautiful woven notes he has progressed to thinking in separately moving harmonies whose blending, to the ordinary sensibility, is more questionable. . . . We in England are especially prone to the danger [of intellectualization in music] because our national sensibility to music is not fastidious, and if we can find an intellectual excuse for a thing we have no sufficient restraining nature to keep us from it. We forgo the desire to please our ears in the desire to please our minds. . . . Where one would condemn a composer who had never got beyond the stage of rough writing, one feels with a composer such as Holst whom one has admired and revered for the felicity and purity of his earlier style, that one cannot wholly condemn; one can merely question and . . . put in a plea for the unintellectual view.

Of great interest here is the fact that both critics appear to champion the non-intellectual view. *The Times* seems to damn with faint praise the formal propriety of the Stanford work, and with it the purely technical approach to appreciation. The critic exhorts the listener to take risks with the composer who, essentially, is feeling his way toward something new. The critic for the *Manchester Guardian* points to the theoretical aspect of composition as seductive but somewhat off the truer goal of artistic sensation and a more intuitive experience. In redefining the terms of the contrast, the latter points to another division: between the conservative and the radical. For the *Guardian* the radical composer is an intellectual; the conservative, therefore, is the truer artist. For *The Times* the definitions are exactly opposite. Furthermore, it is the analytical act carried out by the *Guardian* critic – pointing out the similarity of the grouping of movements to a classical symphony – that is so constraining for the critic of *The Times*. Both, however, recognize the radical nature of the suite, and each lines up on a side almost as a matter of ideology.

Judgments by the reviewers of the press of the early performances (those before the official première of 15 November 1920) tended to fall on either side of this critical fence, though a few straddled it or refused to commit themselves. The reasons for being against or for the work are not so easily disentangled. Coming out against it were *The Globe* ("Noisy and pretentious"); *The Sunday Times* ("Pompous, noisy and unalluring"); *Westminster Dispatch* ("Lacks profundity"); and an early *Times* review ("A great disappointment. Elaborately contrived and painful to hear"). *Saturday Review* got in two shots, calling it "detestable music" after the 27 February 1919 performance, and after the 22 November concert suggesting that "amidst [*The Planets*'] erratic course a good many ears lost their way." A similar wry comment came from the *Morning Post*: "Holst would seem to represent [the planets] in their afflicted aspects."

Balancing these negative reviews were a number of hearty endorsements. The *Westminster Gazette* maintained that "some very strong and original music is contained in the suite. . . . It certainly made good in the purely musical sense. As a whole the work must certainly be reckoned as one of the most remarkable which have come from a native pen." *The Star* granted it "uncommon ability and, above all, genuine imaginative power." In comparing the work to compositions by Busoni on the same program, the *Pall Mall Gazette* (24 Nov 1919) proclaimed it "music of another kind, vividly clear and full of life." *The Times* (24 November 1919) stated unequivocally that it was "the first music by an Englishman we have heard for some time which is neither conventional nor negligible, which stands on its feet and moves its hands and knows what it is doing and where it is going – which is strong and capable." A number of reviewers, such as L. Dunton Green, called for a complete performance of the suite, greatly anticipating its absolute success.

Always complicating the issue is the fact that each performance comprised a different grouping of movements. Some reviewers – and here again L. Dunton Green should be mentioned – apparently knew the entire work, probably having been invited to one of Holst's two piano performances at St. Paul's School. It is perhaps these critics who are most vocal in calling for a complete performance.

The première of the complete suite, by the London Symphony Orchestra under Albert Coates, appears to have left the London music world breathless. Reviews are not simply positive, they are lavish in their praise. Edwin Evans, in *The Outlook* (27 November 1920), called the performance "the most important of recent events in the concert world." In discussing the work Evans points out what he believes makes the work great: its directness and intensity of expression, and its lack of German rhetoric. Evans saw Holst's use of sonority, i.e. its abstract musicality, as the source of emotional expression. Holst, he said, avoided the German need for glib and formalistic logic, letting his "extraordinary sense of tone values" speak directly to the listener. The work has no German conventions of form and grammar to get in the way of immediate communication, which leads to the suite's great intensity. For Evans, this accounted for "much of the success [of the work], for an English audience has always been more easily impressed with intensity than with eloquence in speech." Needless to say, the term "eloquence" refers, in music, to the abundant figuration of such works as tone poems, which for some critics was but glib and superficial decoration. Holst had often been programmed against Strauss's works and reviews for even his early orchestral works, for example *Two Songs Without Words* (1906), compared him favorably in light of the German master's long-winded approach. Ultimately, the most significant praise from Evans – and his praise goes on for several hundred words – occurs when he says that

in each movement of *The Planets* there is thought, clearcut and uncompromising, with no other adornment than that which grows out of itself. In place of the emotional nakedness of the Romantics which was largely literary, Holst, whose elaborations are strictly musical, gives us the severity of the classic nude, which is much nearer to the ultimate ideals of music than even the greatest Romantics have taken us.

Ernest Newman, in *The Sunday Times* (21 November 1920), was equally enthusiastic, calling Holst's "one of the subtlest and most original minds of our time. It begins working at a musical problem where most other minds would leave off." As to the power and effectiveness of the music, he opined that

after a work of this sort the harmonic experiments of the later Stravinsky seem comically infantile. Holst does it all without trying; Stravinsky wants to but can't. . . . [In] his general calculation of effect Holst is astoundingly sure. The vocal finale of *Neptune* is at once one of the most daring pieces of modern writing and one of the most effective.

This is a great contrast with Newman's treatment of Schoenberg's *Five Pieces for Orchestra*: "There are some strangely beautiful things in these Five Orchestral Pieces . . . some fumbling, with ideas only half realised. . . . " [2]

Both of these critics articulate a theme of great significance in any study of rhetoric: the clarity and directness of the communication. Comments along this line of thought come up often in the reviews of the première of the suite. The reviewer in *Queen* said that "the inevitableness of his score carries us along with him through harmonic mazes that with another composer might

Table 3.1 List of reviews of early performances of *The Planets*

1 27 February 1919 (London) (Ma, Me, Sa, Ur, Ju)
2 22 November 1919 (London) (Ve, Me, Ju)
3 10 October 1920 (Birmingham) (Ma, Ve, Me, Sa, Ju)
4 15 November 1920 (London) (première of full suite)

P = Positive review; N = Negative review; M = Mixed; O = Neutral;
PP = Extremely positive review; NN = Extremely negative review;
x/x = two reviews or preview/review

Periodical/Newspaper	1	2	3	4
Arts Gazette	P	P		
Athenaeum				P
Birmingham Gazette & Express			P	
Birmingham Mail			P	
Birmingham News			O	
Birmingham Post			N	
Daily Chronicle	P	O		
Daily Express	P			
Daily Herald		P		
Daily Mail		M	P	P/PP
Daily News (and Leader)		N		P
Daily Telegraph		P		PP
Evening News	O			
Evening Standard (and St. James Gazette)		O		O
The Globe	N			N
Ladies' Field		M		
Manchester Guardian	M		M	P/P
Monthly Musical Record				PP
Morning Post	P			
Musical Opinion			P	
Musical Standard			N	
Musical Times	O			
The Observer		N		O/P#
The Outlook				PP
Pall Mall Gazette	P	P		
Queen				P
The Referee	N/M*			
Sackbut				NN
Saturday Review	N	N		P
The Star	P			
The Sunday Times	N			PP
Sunday Evening Telegram	P			
The Times	N/P+	P		M
Truth				NN

Table 3.1 (*cont.*)

Periodical/Newspaper	1	2	3	4
Westminster Dispatch	N			
Westminster Gazette	P			
Yorkshire Post	M*			

* *The Referee* (23 February) was negative; (2 March), using language identical to *Yorkshire Post* (28 February), was mixed.
+ *The Times* (28 February) was negative; (8 March) was positive.
# *The Observer* preview was neutral; the review was positive.

bewilder, or at least puzzle, us; but which in Holst's case seemed quite natural and logical, so completely is everything 'in the picture' – clear and well ordered." Thus, the "German" logic which Evans found alien to the English character is supplanted by a "natural," though still purely musical, approach.

Another critic, Richard Capell of the *Daily Mail*, made an analogy with "the plain language of our Georgian poets and their reaction against the florid Swinburnian times. It is not poetic and not picturesque – blessedly – but sheer music." Once again there is the reference to pure music, with a logic different both from the poetics and picturesqueness of programmaticism and from the old German formalistic logic. *The Planets*, then, serves, for these critics, as a model of a new modernism – more mature than the French and Russian schools typified by Stravinsky, and more directly expressive than the new German schools led by Strauss and Schoenberg.

The force of this defining event is made clear by the fact that virtually all reviews were positive, with the papers which first offered negative comments changing their verdicts. The *Daily Mail* was one, though it is likely, from a study of the language of the reviews, that it was a change of critic which made the difference; for Richard Capell was clearly a proponent of Holst's musical ideas and would remain a steadfast defender when the composer's later works were misunderstood. *The Referee* likewise seems to have used a different person for the review of this performance, resulting in a complete about-face. But others, such as the *Guardian* and *Saturday Review*, mention their change of heart now that the complete suite was heard as intended. Only *The Globe* maintained its position against the work, though this time it softened the blow: "If Mr. Holst had failed in a sincere attempt . . . the fault was doubtless ours and not his."

Mention must be made of the two truly scathing attacks from *Truth* and *Sackbut*, primarily for the clear difference between the reviewers' thoughts and the description of the audience's response. Both reviewers had much to say about individual movements – and in particularly petty ways:

The whole work gives one the impression of being an anthology of musical platitudes laboriously compiled from the pages of nearly all the prominent modern composers. . . . In the "Jupiter" section we have good examples of Korsakov's style, in "Mercury" an echo of Stravinsky. "Uranus, the Magician" appropriately invokes the familiar strains of Dukas' *L'Apprenti Sorcier*, while in "Neptune" we were treated to a bevy of Debussy's sirenes signalling theatrically from the organloft. Even after they had gone out, shutting the door behind them with an audible click, they continued to exhale their colourless melismata through the keyhole. These may seem hard words, but one cannot stand by unmoved while a perfectly inoffensive and, on the whole, well-meaning cosmos is butchered to make a policeman's holiday.

Sackbut

[Mars] turned out to be our old friend Hagen equipped with a few 5/4 bombs and modern gas appliances, and Venus . . . a placid and thoroughly domesticated personage. Mercury . . . came to the rescue of the somewhat mystified audience with a sparkling concoction of Stravinsky cum Mendelssohn. Jupiter Cambrinus was cleverly snapped in the act of quaffing a pint of four-bar ale, Saturn discoursed amiable Parcifallacies on the subject of senile decay; and when Uranus, tired of the high life, came down and jigged to the tune of our famous national ditty "Tonight, tonight, we will have a night tonight, we will" a tremor of astrological emotion ran through the entire audience. . . .

Truth

This bitter invective hints at some deeper issue, and the enthusiastic response of the audience was more than the reviewers could accept:

It is enough to make one utterly despair of the future of music in this country that after a whole hour of blatant vulgarity and pretentious bombast the entire audience should rise to greet this latest immortal with tumultuous applause that far eclipsed in volume and intensity that which was accorded to such a superlative masterpiece as the *Totentanz* of Liszt, so magnificently rendered earlier the same evening by Siloti.

Sackbut

Is the vox populi always vox Dei? I hope not, for if the vox of the particular populus that thronged the Queen's Hall . . . is at all indicative of the trend of musical opinion in this country, then those of us who have the cause of British music at heart . . . must lower their standards. . . . I can only fall back on the subtle influence of astrology to account for the enthusiasm aroused by this blatant orchestral farrago. . . . Mr. Holst's laborious stitching and unstitching and restitching of patches of half a dozen or more of the best known modern composers . . . amounts to very little from an artistic point of view. To acclaim a work of this kind as a masterpiece of the first rank, as most of the London critics have done, is to render the cause of British music a signal disservice.

Truth

Edwin Evans had called *The Planets* the model of the "New Dispensation"; but, for these two critics at least, the suite was a violation of more sacred trusts: the new German school of Liszt and the "old" English school of Elgar. Nearly all of the other reviews of the première recount the astounding reception given the work and its composer, comparing the event to Elgar's earlier conquest of London.

The reviews for the first American performance a few weeks later in Chicago (it was given simultaneously in New York) were not so effusive. While they recognized the stature of the suite as an example of modern music, there was none of the counterpoint of views which characterize the London reviews. This suggests that, in England, more was at stake. This is a clear distinction between the music worlds of Europe and the United States, for in America the European scene was imported and, as in a museum, put on display. To revere the masterpieces of the past was to be cultured; to take in the novelties of the present was to be current. In London, Holst's suite forced the issue of modernity, demonstrating an alternative to the German hegemony. His experiment was all the more bold for its inclusion of "socially" disparate styles. To be overwhelmed by the music was intoxicating, and for a while England could revel in a new, home-grown, international "star."

As a celestial body, the suite was a "supernova," its effulgence heralding a quick decline. Between 1921 and 1926, Holst collected reviews for seventy-five performances in England. There were many others on the Continent and in the USA. Two recordings were made during this time, and many of Holst's other compositions were revived. However, Holst's newer works were not in the same vein as *The Planets*. They were written with a great austerity of expression, and, while exhibiting a stronger and more consistent technique, they were of a style beyond immediate comprehension. Consequently, the composer simultaneously lost his popularity with the general public and gained credibility with forward-looking critics for his newer style. In both cases, the reputation of *The Planets* suffered. *Mars*, which had so captured the imagination as an expression of war, was by 1930 being called "Holst at his weakest." A few years earlier, Bernard van Dieren called the movement trite. Such criticism is bound to occur and, while it reflects a change in attitude,

37

it also suggests that the work was still in the public mind. It was more ominous that Francis Toye, in an article critical of Holst's tone poem *Egdon Heath* (1927), referred wistfully back to the wonderful power and brilliance of *Beni Mora* (1909–10), overlooking *The Planets* completely.[3] Holst's new, tougher idiom made the experiments in *The Planets* seem clumsy and even immature. At best, the suite was relegated to "middle period" status, as in Harvey Grace's discussion in *The Musical Times* for January 1939. In this view, Holst's later works had so far surpassed *The Planets* that they constituted a third period of great maturity, similar to Beethoven's late compositions. And what appeared to be a revival, in the 1940s, of critical interest in the suite, the chapter devoted to it in Bernard Shore's *Sixteen Symphonies*, turns out to be a reprint, in embellished form, of Richard Capell's article published in *Music & Letters* in October 1927.

Imogen Holst's biographical and critical efforts on behalf of her father focused more on the credibility of his compositional career in general, and on the later and less well known works in particular. This has led to a renewed interest in the late orchestral works which is well deserved. Yet, in light of the bolder tonal excursions of Britten and Tippett, *The Planets* has become more an historical curiosity than a musical force. Nevertheless, a look at the recording history of the suite and its various movements substantiates it as firmly established in the symphonic repertoire and as a part of the general culture. And for a listening public uninitiated in the arcane world of serialism and post-modern experiments it continues to provide a powerful musical experience.

This final point was never questioned; the work was always marked for popular success, and the choosing of favorite movements by reviewers points to Holst's essential accomplishment. The composer was able to focus on the crux of each human characteristic and to search out the most effective method for expressing it. The resulting high contrast of idioms gave greater relief to each movement, intensifying the impression made by each successive *Planet*. His skill as an orchestrator and as a "Tonkunstler" enabled him to individualize each character while creating a subliminal continuity of musical gesture and formal principle throughout the entire work.

The popular success of *The Planets* is a testament to this accomplishment. The concentration, within each movement, on the musical details of character consistently produced favorites as well as arguments for and against each *Planet*. *Mars* seems to have been the most immediate, as well as the most controversial; *Mercury* appears to have caught the imagination most thoroughly and delightfully; *Jupiter*'s festive nature resulted in its consistent use as finale in partial performances, and its central theme quickly achieved, in the British mind, nationalistic qualities. Many critics favored *Saturn* as the most profound and beautiful; and *Uranus* was welcomed as a brilliant scherzo. *Venus* was often criticized, but it had at least one vocal advocate in R. O. Morris who, writing in the *Athenaeum*, called it "fine music" and the most beautiful of all the *Planets*. *Neptune*, quite naturally, seems to have been the least understood, though many found the ending breathtakingly effective.

Perhaps it was the sheer wealth of material, a diversity and range which made delight possible for almost all tastes and levels of appreciation. On the other hand, it is clear that the first full performance had a much greater impact on the critics' appreciation than had earlier partial productions. The sharp contrast between movements brought each character into focus. Regardless of likes or dislikes, the reviewers almost always dealt with what they perceived as the accuracy of the music in portraying character. Some were irked at Holst's choice of personality for a particular *Planet*, but there is always the sense that the reviewers' disgruntled comments were caused by the intensity of Holst's treatment and his ability to create an aura of reality which was highly persuasive.

4

The character plots (1): Mars *to* Mercury

When Holst chose his titles and subtitles he was not indulging in the common form of program music in which a story is told or a scene depicted through sound. The few words he used for titles were meant as suggested characterizations: hints regarding what each musical movement embodied. In a letter to music critic Herbert Thompson, the composer asked him to bear in mind

that the pieces were suggested by the astrological significance of the planets and not by classical mythology – Venus for instance has caused some confusion through this point. Also the tune in Jupiter is *not* a) Keltic [*sic*], b) obviously Irish, c) obviously Greek, d) obviously Russian, e) The Wearing of the Green, f) Polly Oliver, as certain critics have maintained. . . . It is there as a musical embodiment of ceremonial jollity.[1]

The titles, then, were not intended as hints concerning mythological tales. However, by using the names of the planets, and in an order which suggests an outward journey into the unknown, Holst was able to prepare the listener in a certain way, to point the audience in the proper direction. Furthermore, his insistence on astrological cues, in spite of many reviewers' stress on an *astronomical* point of view, was a means of emphasizing the human aspect. Note that, in the letter to Thompson, Holst speaks of astrological significance, not the character of each planet. The implication is that the music is not about the planets; it is about *human* character, for which planetary influence is but the ruling metaphor.

We should not at this point conclude that *The Planets* is simply a collection of musical pictures from which one might pick several for an evening's amusement. The seriousness of most of the movements, as well as their general intensity, speaks against the possibility of caricature. Remember also that the suite was intended to be heard in its entirety. Holst spoke of the movements as being a series of mood pictures, each acting as a foil to the others,[2] and there is indeed a musical variation process which links the movements together in their specified order. So the outward journey implied by the order of movements is paralleled by a psychological journey, and a philosophical one as well: from the physical world to the metaphysical.

How, then, does *The Planets* work as a musical composition, and what part does astrology play? Holst said he had derived his characters from his astrological studies. The book we know Holst owned and used, Alan Leo's *What Is a Horoscope and How Is It Cast?*, was not simplistic in its statements on planetary influence. Not only did it distinguish between various planetary roles (rising vs. ruling planets, etc.) but it also maintained the importance of the relationship of the planets to the signs of the zodiac. Since Holst actually made a hobby of casting horoscopes, the interrelatedness of many aspects must have formed the context for his thinking as he developed his musical characters. When he stated that the individual *Planets* acted as foils to one another, he was only restating this astrological context. In this sense the entire composition is a single human experience in which planetary influence and relationship point to the psychological journey.

In musical terms, the figures presented in each movement partake of a variety of idioms and logical processes, leading to the projection of specific characters based on both real-world associations and listening psychology. On the whole, however, there is a special unity brought about by each movement's involvement in the main tonal "problem." From one movement to the next, musical figures are transformed by having the main theme (and its problem) put under pressure by "characteristic" gestures and idiomatic conventions. The main theme, as a musical figure, is first heard in the opening measures of *Mars*, and it is seemingly too small to hold up under the weight of such a large treatment. But it embodies the fundamental concept of "tonal" cadence and the psychology of resolution. By the end of the last movement the composer has done nothing less than express an alternative musical universe – the inner sanctum, perhaps, of his own personality.

Taking each *Planet* in turn one can observe the development of each single – yet complex – characterization. Like the calculations for each "house" of a horoscope, each movement of the suite is closely worked out. But Holst is not casting a horoscope here; too many things are left out, including the Sun and the Moon, which are considered planets in astrological calculations. His emphasis is on human character and the psychological drama within, played out through astrological metaphors. Each movement is a portrait of one particular aspect of personality. Holst's *modus operandi* is to use both conventional musical "icons" (stylistic elements conventionally linked with extra-musical experiences, for example brass fanfares and snare drums as "military," etc.) and a strict musical logic to project a characterization which is quickly accessible yet rich and coherent in detail. In order to establish the relationship between astrological significance, particularly as described in Alan Leo's book, and the musical action in each movement of the suite, the individual discussions in this, and the following, chapter will be preceded by quotations from Leo. The study of the music will be organized to clarify the iconic qualities of the musical elements as well as their formal interplay. Allowing astrological metaphor to help establish analytical frames of reference should prove to be the most efficient means of letting the music communicate in the way the composer intended.

Mars: the Bringer of War

Mars becomes ruler over the fate and fortune . . . as these persons will make much of their own fate by impulse, and their strong desire-nature. They are fond of liberty, freedom, and independence, and may be relied upon for courage, and quick response in emergencies. They are generous, confident and enterprising, fond of adventure and progress. They will cultivate ambitious and aspiring tendencies. . . . It will be hard to repress them, and there are indications of their being headstrong and at times too forceful. . . .

What is most notable about Leo's description is that it is quite positive, without mention of a (negative) warrior nature. Of course, there is a longstanding association between Mars and war, but it stems primarily from Roman mythology. Other books on astrology mention that Mars, in relation to certain signs of the zodiac, points to a military prowess; yet, knowing that it was Leo's book which Holst was using at the time of composing *The Planets*, the absence seems more significant. It is perhaps the first indication that astrology was only a jumping-off place; that his own psychological program was already in place.

It was earlier pointed out that *Mars* is not the first astrological planet – Leo opens his list with the Sun, the Moon, and then the planets, in astronomical order, starting with Mercury – so for Holst to begin his composition, as a human portrait, with Mars suggests that he saw the aggressive, physical element as primal. Aggression and tenacity are suggested at once, with the ostinato rhythm in $\frac{5}{4}$ time (see Ex. 4.1).

Constantly repeated, on the single note G, the figure pursues the listener across thirty-nine measures before changing pitch, and then continues until m. 57 before it gives way to other material. It returns in the second half of the movement (m. 110), continuing for forty-eight measures – a total of

Ex. 4.1   Reduction of *Mars*, mm. 1–5

62 per cent of the movement overall. When taken at Holst's marked speed of ♩ at 176 the result is clearly "too forceful." However, the sense is not overtly military at the beginning. The scoring does include timpani (marked *p*), but the dominant timbre is of the *col legno* strings. This is a hushed, nearly unpitched sound – one might almost say unmusical, and metaphorically inhuman.[3] With the experience of the inhuman brutality of the Great War still clinging to their bones, the 1920 audience cannot be faulted for assuming that this movement embodied the horrors of modern warfare; however, Holst could not have imagined this in early 1914 as he finished the movement, so this opening was likely meant to be much more abstract and purely psychological.

A negative aspect is supplied to the character by tonal ambiguity and melodic dissonance. From the first, the melodic figure is problematic. Against the background rhythm the main musical figure is heard: the three-note motive, G–D–D♭, in low woodwinds and horns (Ex. 4.1). The first presentation of the figure (mm. 3–5), given against the ostinato, is open-ended, and the very lack of action combines with the harmonic tritone (D♭ to pedal G) and the tonal dissonance of D♭ (C♯–♮4 in the key of G) to set up a motivation for continuance. Imogen Holst calls the D–D♭ move a sinking back in defeat,[4] but this seems contrary to the sharpness of the function. In fact, the event apparently works as a functional "spring" with sufficient torque to generate the next, more extended phrase. The evidence for this is in the movement of the phrase beyond the point of structural close (on G) to the D♭ above (see Ex. 4.2).

By ending the line on D♭ Holst emphasizes the structural importance of the pitch, as well as its various relationships: minor 2nd (against D) and tritone (against G). This emphasizes to the ear the importance of instability to the character of the movement – something which Alan Leo's description did not suggest. In particular, it is the minor 2nd which constitutes the main action of the entire piece: this interval, alone or formed by a combination of other intervals whose difference is a semitone, will be reorientated, recentered, or

43

Ex. 4.2 *Mars*, bassoon line, mm. 3–16

otherwise recontextualized in an effort either to subvert its authority or to sublimate its dissonance to a higher tonal sphere. The characteristically tonal use of the minor 2nd is as leading tone moving up to tonic. But in *Mars* it is a downward, dissonant progression. This emphasis on dissonance gives a yearning aspect to the music which pushes the piece along. A "strong desire-nature" this may be, but it also gives a negative value to the overall character. By the end of *Neptune*, Holst will have found a way to come to terms with this musical problem, and therefore reach psychological peace.

As *Mars* continues, the musical "problem" is developed beyond the use of the minor 2nd into the tonal sphere. The individual pitches of the opening are harmonized (mm. 17 ff) but the sense of key is sometimes thwarted by deceptive chromatic cadence chords and by hopelessly tangled tonal implications. For example, all four pitches used in the opening measures – G, D, D♭ and A♭ – can be construed as functioning in two keys: G and D♭. Also, the same four functions (1, ♭2, ♯4, 5) are found in both keys.

	G	D	D♭	A♭
G:	1	5	♯4	♭2
D♭:	♯4	♭2	1	5

This is further complicated in mm. 17–24 at which point important sonorities can be perceived as being in the key of D major: G–B♭–D♭(C♯) = D: vii°; A–C♯–G = D: V7. The conventional functions of D, and particularly C♯ as leading tone, pull strongly against the tonal primacy of D♭ while keeping it foregrounded.

These entanglements project a tonal ambiguity, and it is this obscuring of the sense of key which brings a negative value to the proceedings. If we can accept, in this piece, the metaphoric parallel of "key is to tonal music what morality is to human character," then, as tonal areas get confused, the movement takes on a "demoralized" feeling. As this passage continues (mm. 25–39), attempts to resolve tonally are constantly thwarted. Finally, in

44

Ex. 4.3 *Mars*, mm. 45–9

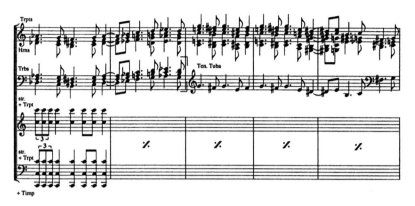

m. 40 (score mark II) the pedal G resolves to C in an apparent triumph of tonal pressure; but the B chord, having alternated with a D♭ chord in its own attempt to come to rest, cannot find the minor 2nd *up* to C and closes on D♭. This D♭ was the errant note in the opening figure and its great clash against the note C projects its tenacity – its bull-headedness. So the cadence at m. 40 explodes under the *fff / tutti* pressure of conflicting melodic progressions and the lack of tonal, and metaphorically moral, stability.

The momentum might have easily disintegrated at this point but, again, as a sign of its too forceful nature, the ostinato pushes on, louder and more aggressive than ever. The D♭ chord also continues, but in a new thematic form (see Ex. 4.3).

The angularity of the first theme gives way to this highly chromatic, snakelike line of parallel chords. Imogen Holst described the horns as "letting their weight slither down . . . ," and there is a further loss of "moral tone" as this theme meanders upward. Tonality is lost, but the melodic progression has nothing with which to make it up. There is a certain momentum: the rhythm is a compression of the opening theme's long–short–long pattern. But tonality now plays almost no conscious part in the development of the character. The lines grope upward with no discernible logic, a musical beast as it were, and would seemingly continue indefinitely except for the interruption at m. 66 and the introduction of the third theme.

Theme 3 (mm. 68 ff, score mark IV) is a battle fanfare which has a striking rhythmic parallel, as Short points out, in Holst's *King Estmere* (1903) (see Ex. 4.4).[5] Going beyond Short's analysis, we find more than a rhythmic similarity: in both fanfares the melody is set at the major 7th above the root

45

Ex. 4.4 (a) *King Estmere*, mm. 2–3 after [14]
(b) *Mars*, mm. 75–6

of the major chord; in both pieces the theme is repeated a number of times in different harmonic settings, with a clear parallel between the climactic setting of each passage. The theme in *King Estmere* is easily heard as a battle motive, bold and confident. Holst may have intended something of the sort here, and the continuation in B♭ (mm. 80–3) is a *tonal* achievement: a clear and confident dominant to tonic cadential figure.

Certain aspects of the opening section carry over. While the ostinato is gone, a repeated quarter-note pulse pounds away under the theme; and the rhythm of the fanfare, quarter notes and triplets, is a transformation of the opening theme. These connections with the first theme encourage a similar association between the clear tonality of mm. 80–3 and the similar tonal focus of mm. 25–8. The triumphant continuation of theme 3 in these measures parallels the rise and fall of tonal presence in the first theme, serving as a reminder that a tonal/moral struggle continues. More needs to be made of these positive elements, as they redirect the character from being an antagonist in the piece to being an emotive complex to which the listener can relate. The almost atonal, negative aspect of the movement now becomes only a part of a larger character; the struggle, metaphorically, is to "save" the total "person" from the consequences of the negative aspect. The preponderance of the negative aspect requires a detailed and extensive solution, but these flashes of tonal confidence establish a more human metaphor, just as the musical information provides the direction for working toward a solution.

For the listener the solution provided by *Mars* is not a comfortable one. As the movement gropes toward its climax there is a great cry of anguish (mm. 167–72, Ex. 5.3*b*), and in the final measures it pounds away, murderously, at the minor 2nd D♭/C. It is not until the final cadence that the dissonance resolves in favor of the note C. But "resolution" is an inaccurate description, as no D♭ actually moves to the final note; D♭ no longer exists. There is no logic in this cadential event, and certainly no elegance. Its brutality is stunning.

Ultimately, the movement *Mars* is not so much 'about war' or its horrors; rather it projects a character which by its very nature brings war on itself. War in this sense is an inner struggle, a trial by fire, a personal ordeal.

The opening ostinato rhythm has been likened to Holst's earlier *Battle Hymn* from *Choral Hymns from the Rig Veda*, Set 1.[6] However, a closer relation is found in *To Agni* (*Choral Hymns from the Rig Veda*, Set 2) which uses an ostinato rhythm in $\frac{5}{4}$, on a single pitch (or chord). The reference is substantiated by the similarity of harmonic device: the progression C: ♭II–I. The text at this point of the hymn ("Burn up our sins, fierce flaming Agni,") reflects the same sense of ordeal as *Mars*, but as a positive value. It is the lack of conventional musical artifice, the lack of tonal logic, in *Mars* which projects a more sinister character.[7]

There is a sense of tenacity and aggression plunging on uncontrolled by a strong moral guidance. The rather glorious transformation of the battle fanfare is disturbing in this context, for there is a chance we will get caught up in it. That the sudden blossoming of tonality should be so quickly swallowed up by more cacophonous and conflicting fanfares is alarming. For an audience firmly grounded in tonal art, the subversion and loss of tonality is a negative – and dangerous – development. And this merging of musical with emotion-laden metaphor is the greatest aesthetic motivation for the existence of the other *Planets*.

Venus: the Bringer of Peace

The beautiful planet Venus is considered the most fortunate star under which to be born. This is probably owing to the even disposition and refined nature of those under this planet's influence. It will awaken in them the affectional and the emotional side of their nature, making them very devoted to those they love. It will also give them a keen appreciation of art and beauty, and stimulate all the pleasure-loving inclinations. . . . [They] love to make all around them happy. . . .

Once again, the subtitle chosen by Holst is drawn from associations for Venus not found specifically in Leo's book. Moreover, unlike the link between Mars and war, the attribute "peace" was not so clearly assigned to Venus in the public mind. *The Referee* (21 November 1920) pointed out that "history has endowed Venus with other attributes which have not always made for peace, but the composer completely ignores these and has written a short movement of delicate character that suggests the pictorial beauties of ancient Greece. . . ." The implication regarding the planet in this review is founded on Roman mythology and recalls the Venus of *Tannhauser*: temptress, seducer, and the cause of wild, profane passion. Holst's *Venus* is perhaps not so far removed from the seductress, whose peaceful existence in Venusberg carried the negative qualities of intoxication. *The Observer* (21 November 1920) wondered about too great a reliance on sensuous tone; and Percy Scholes called it "an expression of sheer beauty rather than of mere peace." But the clear contrast between *Mars* and this movement made the metaphoric opposition of war and peace a natural one.

Overall, this movement sounds much simpler than *Mars*; however, it is characterized by an aesthetic sophistication completely foreign to the first movement. It is the accessibility of the lines, as well as the more conventional tertian harmony, which project simplicity and – after *Mars* – a sense of serenity. The program notes for the 1919 Queen's Hall performance bring up another significant point:

The whole of this movement . . . is pervaded by the serenity of a world which nothing seems able to disturb. The mood is unmistakably *mystical*, and the hero may indeed imagine himself contemplating the twinkling stars on a still night. . . .[8]

The attribute "mystical" may at first seem out of place. None of the reviews at the time used this characterization with regard to *Venus*, perhaps in deference to *Neptune*; yet there is much that binds these two movements together, with the former serving as an imperfect avatar of the latter. The quiet repetition and syncopation of chords, for example mm. 11–19, 32–59, and especially mm. 120 to the end, will return first in *Saturn* and then emphatically in *Neptune*. This fits with the concept of a psychological journey. On the other hand, this mystical element is heard with an increasing timelessness and abstraction as it moves through the later movements, so that in retrospect *Venus* is indeed very sensuous. Thus, while the most likely response to the physical ugliness of *Mars* is to invoke quiet, stillness and a physical beauty, *Venus*'s mystical serenity is only an illusion. And its palpable qualities, so seductive at first, will be made to be heard as weak and insufficient as a resolution of conflict.

The theoretical elegance and relative sophistication are indeed seductive, but the movement represents much more than that. It deals specifically with the issue of minor 2nd resolution. This problem, inherited from the dissonant D♭ in *Mars*, continues to be at the heart of the overall interior, psychological struggle. In following out the interior struggle, the main function of *Venus*, as Imogen Holst says, is "to try and bring the right answer to *Mars*."[9] The music can be followed in this effort both in its iconic presentation (musical symbols of peace) and in its use of musical logic (as opposed to the illogic of *Mars*).

There are several obvious contrasts to *Mars* in this movement: it is quiet, with marks generally between *pp* and *mp* as opposed to *ff* and *ffff*; the orchestration is lighter, often omitting the instruments of the lower register; and the tempo is both significantly slower and much more flexible. The first two elements project the sense of peace as restful and soothing. And when the orchestration expands through the register it envelops the listener with rich diatonic chords. These elements are complemented by the rubato expression which emphasizes the character of the rhythm. The expressive markings in the music are very clear and are much more frequent than in *Mars*. This natural give-and-take of the tempo makes more conscious the shape of the lines, and gives one the sense of a human being carefully and sensitively molding the character of the music. This makes *Mars*, in retrospect, absolutely mechanical and seemingly inhuman. Both movements have long passages of repeated notes, but the gentle rhythmic pulsations in *Venus*, in combination with the major mode, make the lines sweet and languid.

The musical logic also contributes iconically to a certain extent, in its contrast to the apparently illogical meanderings of the earlier movement. But beyond this it must be said that the sense of musical progression in *Venus* is slow and undemanding, allowing it to project restfulness in its own way. The emphasis on subdominant progressions (IV–iii, IV–I) projects a much softer tonal motion. Ultimately, the most significant ramification of tonal logic in this movement is the presence of real cadences and tonal resolution, particularly when they involve the problematic minor 2nd. A prime example is the cadence at mm. 15–16, in which the bass line and harmony produce an upper leading-tone cadence, A♭: ♭II–I (see Ex. 4.5), as the first full cadence of the movement (see Chapter 6).

There is more to *Venus* than a contrast to *Mars*; it has a subtle and complex personality of its own. The opening gesture, a gentle stepwise ascent in the horn, is reminiscent of Wagner's *Siegfried Idyll*, a convenient association supporting the sense of repose; yet the deceptive cadences (mm. 5 and 10) and the lack of tonic presence highlight a sense of yearning similar to – though emotively far removed from – the striving of *Mars*.[10]

The first theme is based almost entirely on the opening horn figure. When the upward line repeats, it is answered (and closed off) by a counterpoint response based on the figure's inversion. *Mars* was lacking this type of response, which is a noticeable point of contrast between movements. The

Ex. 4.5   *Venus*, mm. 13–16

Ab: ii   bII   I⁽⁶⁾

repetition of this answering descending line works toward the full cadence at
mm. 15–16; furthermore, it creates a closing response based on the descending
answer of mm. 3–4, 8–9, and specifically mm. 14–15. This economy intensifies
the experience of the line and purifies its character.

While the first theme has a quiet accessibility, there is a more difficult
harmonic issue: the deceptive cadences and chromatic progressions mentioned
earlier. Each of the first two presentations of the opening theme end in false
resolutions. The first wants to resolve to Eb, but the chord arrived at, in a
perfectly logical manner, is Db minor (i.e. minor bvii)! The second reaches the
same conclusion: Bb minor in place of the implied Cb. There is a groping
forward here similar to that found in *Mars* with the significant difference that
the particular logic of the lines here relaxes the tension and encourages a faith
in the intuitive nature of *Venus*.

The chromaticism continues to be felt strongly at the higher structural levels
(as discussed in Chapter 6), but the effect is always ameliorated by linear
considerations. For example, the move into the second theme (mm. 27–32)
progresses from the key of Bb minor to F# major, and chordally from Bb minor
to B major with a major 7th! Yet the sound is quite natural for two reasons:
the chord progression is Bb: i→II, a simple reversal of the cadence formula in
mm. 15–16 which can also be heard simply as F#: iii–IV; and the note Bb is
both the final of the previous melody and the opening (as A#) of the new theme.

The second theme, with its strong subdominant emphasis, is both serene and
yearning. This latter quality is emphasized by the successive "waves" of the
theme, constantly returning in slight variation and recombination as it seeks
its resolution. While the subdominant will generally soften the tonal
motivation of a theme, here the tonic never actually appears in its first
presentation. This intensifies the yearning at the very point where the *Mars*
issues are raised, for it is in this theme that variants of the first-movement
themes occur. Of particular import is the semitone slip at mm. 46–7. The
acoustic resonance of the scoring masks the extreme tonal dissonance, but it

50

Ex. 4.6   *Venus*, mm. 67–72

is, metaphorically, only a forced solution to the minor 2nd problem. While it is delicious at the moment, it will be surpassed in both logic and sweetness in *Neptune*.

Holst was exceedingly clever in the organization of this second theme, balancing the easy triadic harmony and slow harmonic rhythm with surprising turns of phrase and chromatic substitutes for dominant chords. As the theme seemingly plays itself out, the composer introduces a new, almost too sweet romantic gesture. It arrives at mm. 67–8, shifting suddenly from F♯ to F. The shock is prepared, of course, by virtue of the keys and pitches (violins: C♯–C) being further examples of the semitone slip. The ensuing harmonic progression is senseless at first glance: F major, G–5 (major with a diminished 5th), B major over a D♭, D♭ augmented, B♭ major over a C. But the logic is aurally impeccable (see Ex. 4.6).

The suppleness of voice-leading and harmonic motion is a major contributor to the emotive aspect of this movement. Since this enticing progression deals with the issue of resolving the minor 2nd it takes on a significance beyond itself: it is a working out of a "right answer."

The final aspect of character is projected by the orchestration at the end of the movement.[11] The use of static repeating figures in harp and celesta, and the use of high "bodiless" registration, is a metaphor of "heavenly" and "ethereal." The closing chord is an E♭ major with added 6th, and the highest pitch of the sonority is the melodic C. The added note, C, has both acoustic and theoretical ramifications. It gives a sparkle to an otherwise dull major chord, but it also is a structural link with *Mars* which ended on C. Here it finds rest in the upper atmosphere.

51

Mercury: the Winged Messenger

Known as the "winged messenger of the gods," [Mercury] is a favourable planet to those who have left the senses for the mind; but as a ruling planet much always depends upon the aspects which it received from other planets, its mercurial nature being such that it absorbs much of the planet with which it comes into contact, it being in a word what we may term a convertible planet. . . . Mercury is itself colourless. . . . But apart from this, Mercury gives adaptability, fertility of resource, and the ability to use the mind in various ways. . . .

Finally, Holst uses an attribute given in Leo; however, ironically, it is also borrowed from Roman mythology! Perhaps the composer, himself a Mercurian, enjoyed the conceit that he had this potential locked within him. Holst left the composition of this movement till the very end, and, while he left us no stated reason or cause, he might well have been unsure of his approach. In an earlier letter to Herbert Thompson[12] he said, "As far as I can remember I had the scheme of the Planets roughly worked out in my mind by Easter 1914 except Mercury which was added later." What might have been the reason for his delay in composing this movement?

R. O. Morris provided a possible cause, indirectly, when he opined that in *Mercury* "Mr. Holst approaches the domain of programme music pure and simple. It is not easy to suggest an alternative treatment of the subject, for it is essentially pictorial in idea. Mercury is a mere activity whose character is not defined. We know nothing of him except the swiftness of his movement. . . ." Leo was not much help when he called Mercury essentially colorless. Ultimately, the movement was fitted into the scheme as a scherzo – probably intentionally, but we have no way of knowing – and the program notes for the 22 November 1919 performance (of *Venus, Mercury*, and *Jupiter*) state the case: "The movement takes the place of a scherzo and is mainly constructed [of] the welcome datacompordinary major scale with the four lower notes shifted a semitone upward."

In comparison to the description for *Venus* in these program notes, this is dry and lifeless; yet it does imply, to a certain extent, both the character of the movement and its role in the sequence. If there is something of the joke in *Mercury* it involves the crucial minor 2nd issue inherited from *Mars*. The "curious scale" of *Mercury* not only contains the semitone slip, it can also be analyzed as two tetrads, B♭–C–D–E♭, and E–F♯–G♯–A, which are a tritone apart. This recalls, at least theoretically, the tritone dissonance so obvious at the beginning of *Mars*: G–D♭. Thus, the delicate scoring, the exciting swiftness of the lines, and the clever manipulation of meter disguise the deeper

Ex. 4.7   *Mercury*, mm. 1–5 reduced

musical difficulty of validating the tritone and chromatic sideslip in the tonal realm.

The scoring of *Mercury* was a major source of deserved acclaim. Holst demonstrates a marked ear for color, and by limiting his thematic work to short arpeggio and scale work he makes the *vivace* tempo practical for players with limited rehearsal time. His dovetailing of instruments across registers (for example cello feeding into viola, which feeds into violin II and violin I, then back down again; or bassoon to clarinet to flute [mm. 1–4]) creates the illusion of something both palpable and imagined, of the nimbleness of the thought processes of a genius too quick to follow. The sense of key is developed in the same way. The B♭ and E tetrads and arpeggios hint at the key of A major, but when it arrives, as in m. 4 and m. 28, it disappears before we are sure of our bearings (see Ex. 4.7).

The clever and witty juxtaposition of tritone-related keys, highlighting the tritone, minor 2nd, and perfect 5th, establishes the tangled hierarchy of tonal grammar and demonstrates the dire consequences of an action initiated by a tritone gesture outside its traditional functional role. In this view, *Mercury* parallels the Shakespearean "fool" who always manages to comment significantly on the issues – though indirectly.

The middle section of this "scherzo" is generally traced to *Dance of the Marionette* from Holst's *Japanese Suite* (written just prior to *Mercury*), particularly for its $\frac{6}{8}$–$\frac{3}{4}$ metric interplay.[13] Beyond this, however, there is an harmonic flexibility (a Mercurial attribute) in the way tonic C is maintained through the series of diminished chords and Mixolydian implications. Overall, the section forms a stable tonal oasis between two restless expanses. Its most obvious characteristic is its dance nature, and it seems related in this aspect to the third movement of *Beni Mora*, *In the Street of the Ouled Nails*. In the latter movement a short ostinato figure is repeated through the entire length

53

of the piece, creating a mesmerizing effect – an altered state of experience. The swirling repetition of *Mercury*'s middle section is comparable.

The tritone of *Mars* was projected as relentless and negative; tonally it emphasized non-function. *Mercury* has forced a reappraisal of the interval, subsuming it into tonal function (♭2–5) and then suggesting it as a dominant substitute. Ending on E major will make metaphoric sense, when *Neptune* – and the suite – does so, as the key of "solution." *Mercury*, as metaphor of "flexibility," has projected that concept tonally and given both the tritone and its sense of ambiguity a positive value.

5

The character plots (2): Jupiter *to* Neptune

Jupiter: the Bringer of Jollity

This will give an abundance of life and vitality. Those born under its influence are cheery and hopeful in disposition, and possess a noble and generous spirit. . . . This planet confers fortune and success upon all his children. . . . [They] possess that true religious spirit which gives faith, and abundant hope.

It is curious that Holst, in looking for a word to express "abundance of life and vitality," chose "jollity" rather than "joviality" for his subtitle, the latter being derived from "Jove," Jupiter's other name in mythology. In fact, several early reviewers mistakenly used "joviality" when they gave subtitles in their articles. On the other hand, the *Oxford English Dictionary* gives a much richer history for the composer's choice and a range of meaning which covers both joyous merrymaking and magnificent splendor. Also, it may be that Holst wished to avoid reference to the established astrological adjective, "jovial"; for the planet was not to bring the attributes of the *mythological* personage, but was to point toward *human* characteristics. In any case, early reviews suggest that the movement communicated quite clearly the attributes associated with the planet in astrology.

Vitality is evident in *Jupiter* from the opening waves of sixteenth notes and the energizing syncopations of the opening theme (Ex. 5.1*a*). The *pesante* theme at m. 65 (Ex. 5.1*d*) is dangerously close to a vaudeville finale, but it carries forward the jocular trochees which precede it (mm. 47–8, mm. 55–6; see Ex. 5.1*c*), and Holst's orchestral treatment develops the character continuously. The theme at m. 108 (Ex. 5.1*e*) – characterized by reviewers as a folktune – is a rustic dance constructed so as to have no end. Its repetitions gather energy through increased orchestration and tempo, whirling recklessly as did the middle dance of *Mercury*. It is unsophisticated and childlike in its content and treatment, to be enjoyed for its physical experience. The noble and religious aspect is carried by the center theme (Ex 5.1*f*), but it is in marked contrast to what has come before. Holst, for the first – and really the

Ex. 5.1   *Jupiter* themes

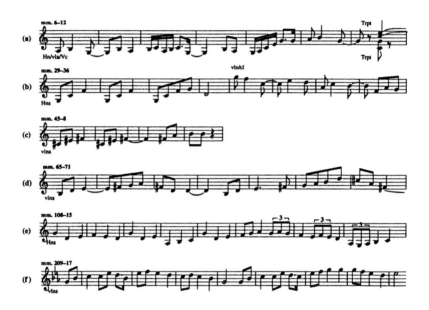

only – time in the whole of *The Planets*, creates a strong rhetorical differentiation within a single movement. Lack of transition between themes further emphasizes the disjunctiveness of styles, and not just at the beginning of the noble theme but between all the themes of the movement, which, in turn, promotes a strong sense of conflict just beneath the surface.

The conflict harkens back iconically to the warrior spirit during what must be called the fanfares, first heard at mm. 29–32 (Ex. 5.1*b*) and developed throughout. These are developed over another battle motive: a military tattoo, based on the rhythm of the opening theme and first articulated in the brass (m. 160), then moving to the timpani and finally to the lower strings. It would probably be wrong to construe this as a recall of the ordeal in *Mars*, as the context is for the most part festive. On the other hand, *Jupiter*'s musical structures and generative processes not only recall metaphors of *Mars*, but of other *Planets* as well.

For example, the theme at m. 45 (Ex. 5.1*c*) develops in the same way as does the opening of *Mars*: a small (three-note) motive, repeated as part of an upward extension reusing the motivic outline. The opening material presents evidence for two different keys, A minor (coming out of *Mercury*'s final E) and C major, and handles the tonal implications with a flexibility reminiscent of that previous *Planet*. This is true also of the center theme at m. 193. There the thematic outline points toward C minor while the overall texture is presented in E♭ major. This tonal sleight of hand is no longer witty, as it might have been in *Mercury*; rather it has become part of the larger emotional character of the entire suite, up to this point. The center theme also has a yearning aspect, for its last phrase is open, with dominant harmony, leading back into its opening phrase at the next higher octave. The second theme in *Venus* yearns in a similar way, but perhaps closer is the opening of *Mars* whose three-note figure steadily climbs upward without reaching its desired resolution. Finally, the unexpected *lento maestoso* at mm. 388–93, which reprises the center theme, gives a glimpse of the future in its use of *Neptune*'s texture and the hint of the key of G♯ minor.

These conflations notwithstanding, the mood of *Jupiter* is celebratory and climactic. There is hidden irony here as Holst places this movement only halfway through his journey. The success of Jovians would be, for Holst, empty because it is too physical. On occasion, he warned against public success, saying that it robbed a person of a purer motivation. He had once said to Clifford Bax: "Some day I expect you will agree with me that it's a great thing to be a failure. If nobody likes your work, you have to go on just for the sake of the work. . . . Every artist ought to pray that he may not be 'a success'."[1] This attitude, joined with the fact that the movement ends only the first half of the suite, suggests that Holst did not see the celebration in *Jupiter* as conclusive; it is but one aspect of the ultimate character. It is doubly ironic that this *Planet* would play so big a part in giving him the fame he truly feared.

Saturn: the Bringer of Old Age

The planet Saturn as lord and ruler makes the progress through life slow and steady. Those under its influence will be more plodding and persevering than brilliant and active. They have a firm hold on life and should live to an advanced age. Whatever they do will be thorough and enduring. They are likely to lose opportunities through not being responsive enough, and appearing too diffident and cold. They are very faithful . . . , but are undemonstrative and rarely if ever enthusiastic. They are more inclined to action than speech, and with them actions speak louder than words. . . .

This description is so close to the composer's personality, as depicted by his biographers, that we might easily assume this was his own ruling planet. He said that this was his favorite movement in the suite, and perhaps this was a preference based on emotional as well as technical grounds. The hold it had on him extended well into the future, for its B minor theme was to be the basis of the processional theme in *Egdon Heath* (1927), his favorite among his own works, and his acknowledged "masterpiece."

From the first performances of *Saturn*, its iconic value was very strong for listeners, though emotional interpretations varied somewhat. That is to say, everyone heard "old age" in the music, but some heard it negatively while others construed it more positively. Through the years, the metaphor of the subtitle has generally been interpreted by the main commentators (Imogen Holst, Edmund Rubbra, and Michael Short) to mean desolation. Imogen does acknowledge the ending as having a mood of acceptance, but she heard it as an acceptance of human tragedy.[2] There is also the reference made to the passing of time and the aging process, the tireless counting out of the minutes as they pass by, and the peaceful resignation of the ending. Short mentions the ending as a transformation of the opening material, and the iconic value of the material is emphasized for all of the commentators throughout the piece: the opening alternating chords are the ticking of a clock; the long notes are dragging limbs. However, there are other musical signs at work here.

The slow tempo suggests the slower pace of the aged, but the insistence on a steady alternation of half-note values through most of the piece projects a plodding character. This is supported by the long-tone opening melody (Ex. 5.2*a*), the slow quarter-note bass line undergirding the B minor theme (Ex. 5.2*b*) beginning at m. 28, and the use of steady bass and timpani off-beat accompaniment to the four-flute tune starting at m. 50. This last tune has also been characterized as cold and arid. Even as this melody is shifted to the brass and becomes louder its force is more from determination and perseverance than from brilliance.

The musical grammar also supplies metaphors. The opening oscillating half-diminished chords hold tonal progression in abeyance, a symbol of timelessness. This is true also of the repeating, and therefore static, ostinato at m. 28, and of the repeating and cascading texture of the whole last section (mm. 105–55) as well. There is also, finally, a progression in the large-scale tonal realm and in the texture (mm. 38 ff) which creates a sense of narrative. Other possible emotive associations include the long-note melody at the end (mm. 125 ff), which is stable (strong) and ascending (a positive value), and which projects a note of triumph such as is heard in the finale of Mahler's Second Symphony ("Resurrection"). The movement of the melody from the low register to the upper (from the opening section through m. 46) and its gradual transformation from atonal (or at least unstable) to tonal perspective is also

Ex. 5.2   Comparison of versions of *Saturn*, theme 1

a positive value. And, while the melody at the end is heard in the lowest register, it is balanced in the high register by cascading flutes and harps and bells.

The narrative aspect comes to the foreground in this movement because the reprise is so clearly transported beyond, rather than a reversion to, the starting point. The opening chords are unstable and without resolution, while the last section is dominated by extended tonics: E major (mm. 105–13), and C major (m. 125 to the end of the movement). The opening melody (first in the basses, mm. 4–12) focuses on the tritone, while the closing presentation of that theme centers on the perfect 4th. The opening pitch collection, forming a synthetic scale (B–C–D–E♭–F–G–A–B), contributes to the feeling of instability as the movement begins, and is contrasted at the end with clear diatonicism. The progression from instability to stability is worked out overtly through the movement. The opening theme (mm. 4–7, Ex. 5.2*a*) is transformed in the B minor version (Ex. 5.2*b*, *c*, *d*) – itself a progression from minor (Dorian) to major mode – and finally in the major-mode treatment in the last section of the piece (Ex. 5.2*e*). And, true to a narrative format, before the final transformation, the original version is recalled (mm. 84–7, all low instruments) and put under pressure to change.

This recall of the opening theme is perhaps the most remarkable episode of the movement, for it is set in such a way as to bring back an equally pressurized moment in *Mars* (see Ex. 5.3).

59

Ex. 5.3 (a) *Saturn*, mm. 88–93; (b) *Mars*, mm. 167–72

The yearning long tones and dissonances push through successively lower registers as they exhaust themselves through a persistent but seemingly vain reiteration. The result in *Mars* is the brutal final cadence; in *Saturn* it is the resolution into E major.

This acknowledgement of a Martian character in *Saturn* is based on a much deeper relationship of themes and the tritone/minor 2nd issue: the opening theme's tritone–semitone–semitone figure is a revision of the Martian perfect 5th–minor 2nd gesture.[3] It is also supported by at least one other iconic passage: the second half of the four-flute tune. The tune is presented twice, first with four flutes over a quiet accompaniment (mm. 54–65) and then with fuller accompaniment and culminating in trumpets and horns on the four-part theme (mm. 66–77). The first version is a somewhat somber processional, its simple, stoic contour distorted by chromatic harmony. As the second presentation gets under way it gradually becomes a march. The pure triads heard in the brass become more like a fanfare, but the chromatic relations between chords has a wrenching effect, giving this part of the movement something of the negative value associated with *Mars*. The final narrative result is the recognition that the closing serenity is reached only through the ordeal of *Mars*.

With this in mind, *Saturn* becomes the most human of the movements. Not only does it have rich details of character, it has a sense of growth; and most surprising of all it has memory, through which the ordeal of growth becomes a transformation. By the end of the piece, the oscillating major 2nds, which have been heard since the beginning, take on the serenity of *Venus* as they copy the oscillating figure from that movement. The added 6th on the E major cadence chord (m. 105) and the C major cadence chord (m. 125) both recall the final section and cadence chord in *Venus*. So the old age of *Saturn* is enriched by the extremes of the opening *Planets* as it projects a more fully human serenity.

Uranus: the Magician

The mystic planet Uranus will affect the major portion of the life of those who come under the higher influence of Aquarius. . . . It will bring them into touch with original and unique experiences; inclining them always toward the metaphysical . . . , tending to stimulate in them all the higher side of human, intellectual and finer nature. When leaning toward the adverse and material side of this influence, persons will be eccentric, strange and erratic; but it may be that this will be induced by others who cannot understand their way of viewing things. Sudden and unexpected events will enter into their lives. . . . They will be very independent and unique characters, possessing a nervously organized temperament quite out of the common.

The first half of this quotation from Leo's book seems to fit Holst's *Neptune* better than its does his *Uranus*. It is perhaps a surprise to see the appellation "mystic" applied here, and it is one more indication that the composer is happy to sacrifice astrological accuracy in favor of his own psychological program. The materials and progression of *Uranus: the Magician* were spoken of, by the early reviewers, as eccentric and not a little silly – attributes which match Leo's description of the Uranian who leans "toward the adverse and material side" rather than the "higher" and "finer" side of human nature. Some of this may have been the result of the critics finding a parallel for the movement in Dukas' *L'Apprenti Sorcier*, but Holst employs a variety of compositional tactics (strongly physical rhythmic gestures, obvious metric syncopation, and surprising tonal digressions) which might support this description.

In pursuing the erratic and eccentric, he may have seized an opportunity, as Imogen believed, to resurrect the bizarre but humorous world from the *Phantastes Suite* which he had buried after its first performance in 1912. So the "bumbling wizard" takes center stage. The subtitle "Magician" implies the occult world, even if the music does not, further encouraging the comparison made with Dukas' piece. The musical parallels between the two works are not as great as *The Times* reviewer of 16 November 1920 would have us believe ("it was difficult to escape the reminiscence of *L'Apprenti Sorcier* here"). In fact, aside from the feeling of a heavy-footed but rollicking march in triplet time, there is little in common. To be sure, the tunes in both are comic in their simple-mindedness (though Holst's movement has more tunes and a greater range of characterization), and both begin with an apparent seriousness before the fun starts. Also, both rely on brilliant orchestration (with Holst's being larger, and more audacious). Both also highlight the bassoon for thematic work in the opening. But these are hardly close enough parallels for an intruding musical reminiscence; on the other hand, it suggests that both pieces were heard principally as brilliantly orchestrated comic relief.

It is at least within the realm of possibility that Holst wrote *Phantastes* as a response to Dukas' work, and when it did not meet his standards he revived the concept within the context of *The Planets*. In any case, Imogen Holst certainly believed in a relationship among these three works sufficient to expand on the metaphors a bit. Her descriptions, however, deal mostly with the comic aspect:

Holst is back again in a region of wizards and their magic spells, and we are made to suffer from some of the blatancies that were left over when "Phantastes" was discarded. The Magician's apprentices hop about in a galumphing six-four. . . . The tune [at m. 72] is a mixture of mock-oriental and mock folk-song, with a flat-footed accompaniment that gets heavier and noisier at each repetition. It is followed by several bars of true comedy as the timpani quotes [*sic*] the galumphing six-four version of the incantation, and the bass tuba replies with the original slow notes which it utters in a subdued and pensive tone of voice. . . .[4]

It is true that these interpretations build up like a house of cards, with little of an objective nature to hold them together. But one can find, as Imogen does, a great deal of the unexpected, the overdone, the unbalanced, and even the eccentric in the music itself. From this point of view the subject of the program is a sort of merry incompetence which is in the scherzo spirit. If this is a magician, the listener might say, then he cannot be a frightening one; his smoke and shrieks come to nothing – I am not intimidated, but I am entertained.

The first theme, for example, might be detailed as follows:

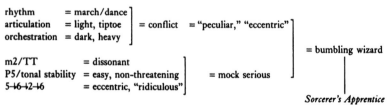

There is a conflict between the lightly tiptoeing figures (alternating

Ex. 5.4   Themes from *Uranus*

eccentrically between $\frac{6}{4}$ and $\frac{3}{2}$) and the "march" character; between the rather silly tune (Ex. 5.4*b*) and the orchestration which ranges from a heavy low to a shrieking high register. This theme follows an opening four-note figure (Ex. 5.4*a*), labelled by Imogen as an incantation. For such a serious, and ominously dissonant, figure to be followed by a dancing, marching, tiptoeing, sometimes shrieking, sometimes tittering creature does suggest a peculiar circumstance.

There is also a discrepancy between the emphasis on dissonant intervals in the opening figures (for example mm. 9–11: e: 5, ♭6, ♭2, ♭6, 5, ♭5, 4, ♭5, 5, using minor 2nds and tritones) and the tonally easier "tunes" (for example mm. 47–51 [Ex. 5.4*b*]). These juxtapositions suggest a mock seriousness and eccentricity of character, and they project, within the context of *L'Apprenti Sorcier* and *Phantastes*, the image of a bumbling wizard.

Likewise, the third theme (mm. 71 ff, Ex. 5.4*c*) begins innocently enough, stepping up through a D major scale, but it quickly proceeds up a semitone to E♭ minor! Always on the brink of tonality, the line takes on a whole-tone character that "misses" its expected tonal goal. The outlandish harmonic progression (I–ii) centers around the unexpected enharmonic pun, F♯/G♭, which is the third scale degree in both keys. The smallest step sends the listener over the tonal precipice, projecting a sense of adventure and tonal recklessness which, in the spirit of the first theme, is roller-coaster-like fun.

Besides the comic element there is a deeper sense of parody which adds a darker twist to the movement. There are elements from earlier movements which undergo a comic transformation. The semitone–tritone combinations which are the basis for *Mars* and *Saturn*, so serious in their original contexts, are literally turned upside down in the tiptoeing figures which fill the opening section here. In *Mars* the figure was G–D–D♭; in *Saturn* it became F–B–C–B; now, in *Uranus*, it is B–C–F–C. When the figure is heard in its tonal context, as noted above, the line becomes a strange comic hybrid – more out of key than in it. What was seen as the cause of a terrible ordeal is now, for this magician, child's play.

Likewise, the second theme (mm. 45 ff, Ex. 5.4*b*) combines the opening figure of *Saturn*'s processional theme with a parody of *Venus*'s third theme (Ex. 4.6). It is not the demonic parody of Berlioz's *Symphonie Fantastique*, yet it lays low all human pretension, mocking as it entertains. The final blow comes in the last theme (Ex. 5.4*d*), a march in which the accompanying rhythmic cadence never quite gets into step and the tune ends with a fanfare in the wrong key. So much for the military character!

At the end of all this Holst found what reviewers considered the perfect unexpected stroke, what Imogen called his "magic" chord: an F9 chord, a soft subdominant in the prevailing key of C. It has a role of great significance in the musical plot of the suite (to be discussed in Chapter 6); metaphorically, it *is* magic in that it is beautiful, cold, and sudden: the wizard, tired of games, disappearing into thin air. Perhaps the wizard is not bumbling after all, but a force so powerful and with a view so wide that he can afford to humor himself, and us. With this statement the issue of autobiography, which arose in the discussion of *Saturn*, must again be addressed. Holst certainly recognized his affinity for the mystical aspect of life, and his natural reticence might have led others to consider that "higher" side of his nature. Yet, in his music, this more physical and audacious side was to continue to show itself, not only in his legitimate works – *The Perfect Fool*, the *Double Concerto*, and *Hammersmith*, for example – but in various school-oriented "skits" such as *Futuristic Tone Poem in H* and *Opera as She Is Wrote*. Both of these poked fun at existing musical conventions and at particular composers (Richard Strauss, Debussy, Wagner, Verdi, and others) with Holst providing stylistic carica-tures which must have often plunged into silliness.[5]

Neptune: the Mystic

... the influence of this planet will be very potent during the major portion of the life of mediums and psychics. The more they come under the planet's influence, the more will their psychic tendencies develop. . . . These persons should endeavour to live as purely as possible, so that they may sense a few of those vibrations that so rarely come to the ordinary human being. . . .

With the planet *Neptune* Holst arrived at a characterization for which his audience was fully prepared, but in which he used a rhetorical approach that was stunningly new. By choosing "The Mystic" as his subtitle the composer had created a link with his earlier "Sanskrit" works. The pristine language of the *Choral Hymns from the Rig Veda*, coupled with the exotic mysticism of their texts, provided a jumping-off point for Holst as well as a metaphorical "key" for the audience. By the time *The Planets* was publicly performed, *The Hymn of Jesus*, with its recognizably mystical text and character, had had its successful première, establishing Holst's reputation for this audience. So the mystical state as the point of final arrival in *The Planets* would make perfect sense. Yet nothing of Holst's that had come before prepared the listener for so musically spare, though immediately recognizable, a presentation of this characterization. The sense of abstraction, of aesthetic "distance," is created for the listener by an absence, to a great extent, of familiar musical language. This was true of *Mars* as well; in that movement, however, the sense of melody and harmonic progression was strong enough to give the listener a basis for intellectual judgment. In this final movement, the absence seems so great as to remove all basis for judgment, which is as precise a parallel to the mystical state as Holst might ever have conceived.

The apparent lack of musical grammar and harmonic motion, and the *Klangfarben* orchestration, are perhaps the most easily identifiable components of this mystical character. Neither of these derive from Holst's previous compositions, so they mark this movement as somewhat different with reference to earlier portrayals of the mystical state (*Choral Hymns from the Rig Veda, Savitri, Dirge and Hymeneal*, for example). The texture of the *Klangfarben* sections is particularly important: sustained chords filled in with very fast passage work. It creates a paradoxical sense of stasis and high activity occurring simultaneously. The voicing of the chords and the instrumental combinations employed result in unusual acoustic properties, with swiftly changing overtone complexes embedded in the sound. Individual instruments lose their identities as they join to project new musical timbres.

Interestingly enough, the basic sonority for the movement is the simple triad. The opening section comprises an alternation of E minor and G♯ minor triads through a short, arpeggio-based melody. Imogen called this oscillation the "effortless hush of deep calm breathing."[6] The complementary material which follows this is diatonic and harmonized in pure triads. These sonorities, as well as the melodies which articulate them, project a restfulness, a serenity mingled with the sadness commonly associated with the minor mode. There is neither enough rhythmic propulsion nor expressive gesture to produce anything approaching human warmth or passion. (Holst marked in the score "play *sempre pp* throughout, dead tone," except for the theme in the final, blissful, major-mode section.) So the mystical state is quickly associated with a stoicism which might pass for melancholy.

The relationship between the opening triads seems to have an exotic or irrational quality, but the voice-leading can also be construed meaningfully in traditional tonal terms: in G♯ minor, G is enharmonic with F✗ (♯7) and E is the flattened 6th.

$$
\begin{array}{ccc}
\sharp 7 & - & 1 \\
\flat 6 & - & 5 \\
\text{g}\sharp: \ \text{vii}°7 & & \text{i}
\end{array}
$$

So this alternative harmonic cadence can be rooted in a traditional progression. The common tone, B, alters the leading chord out of the diminished form and makes the diminished 7th interval, ♯7–♭6, harder to hear: the perfect 5th between E and B stabilizes the E as the root of an E minor chord. But in spite of this difficulty, by m. 16 the G can be heard as a functioning leading tone, resulting in a new harmonic sequence, g♯:♭vi–i. Thus the progression provides a subliminal tonal function which allows the exotic to project a sense of resolution. The use of ♭II–I progressions throughout *The Planets* has been conditioning the listener for just this kind of *sub rosa* tonality, and it returns at the very end to complete the perception of inner peace and fulfillment.

After the opening section Holst begins to merge the simple triads (m. 22): G♯ minor under E minor "resolving" to an open 5th on E under G♯ minor. The first is heard as a rather tense first inversion E chord with both major and minor 3rds and a major 7th; the second is a more restful E major 7th chord in root position. The sonority is somewhat cluttered by the quick-moving filigree in harps and upper strings, but the sense of tension followed by a release is clear (see Ex. 5.5).

This activity continues through m. 44, involving several tonal areas, and provides a replacement for standard tonal function. There are also a number of upward resolving 4ths and downward moving 5ths in the bass to solidify the sense of progression. The normalcy implied by traditional notions of progression aids in the projection of restfulness while the chord fusions increase the energy of the movement.

Figures and devices from other movements are brought back in *Neptune*,

Ex. 5.5 *Neptune*, mm. 22–3, trumpets and trombones

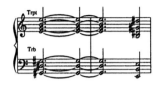

either to be reinterpreted from the mystical perspective, or to affirm the earlier "proto-mystical" elements. The chord fusions might well recall for the listener the D♭–C fusion of *Mars*; however, here the sound is *pp*, and, with the resolving sonority always to follow, the listener can concentrate on the abstract sound of the fusion. On the other hand, the limpid lines – and especially the melody and oscillating major 2nds beginning at m. 58 – harken back to the peace of *Venus*. Likewise, the texture of *Neptune* was first heard at the end of *Jupiter* (mm. 388–92), and then in *Saturn* (mm. 125–45). Also, the change, in *Saturn*, from sad minor-mode themes to the more peaceful major mode parallels the shift in *Neptune*, bringing the earlier sense of blissful serenity with it. Even *Uranus* is brought back, though not in temperament: its closing cadence, F9–E (open), the "magic" chords falling a minor 2nd, is re-created for the ending of this last movement. The gentle oscillation of the two chords, in the lightest possible vocal sonority, accommodates the ear with a subliminal tonal function: ♭II7 (standing for V[♭5♭9 without the root])–I6. The sound, for the general listener, is "right" but inexplicably so; thus, a mystical serenity.

Following Holst's psychological program, this last movement does not depict the traditional psychic medium as much as it does the artist who has lived purely (or at least sincerely) and is thereby launched onto a higher plane of experience. Those who knew of Holst's life – up to that point and then beyond, to the very end – would see a clear parallel in the composer's life with the journey embodied in *The Planets*. This is not to suggest that Holst was so pedantic as to compose a piece to promote his way of life; rather, he simply wrote what he felt as both artist and human being.

6

On becoming *The Planets*: the overall design

The wealth of musical metaphor in each movement of *The Planets* explains the immediate popularity of the work, whether it was heard in its complete form or only in part. Furthermore, the use of different musical idioms within a movement not only added richness to the metaphoric effect, it broadened the audience to which the work might appeal. As mentioned earlier, approval was expressed by all levels of listeners, in provincial cities as well as in London. Anecdotes concerning charwomen dancing in the aisles balanced the more serious comments of reviewers, attesting to its democratic appeal. Holst's use of popular idioms back-to-back with more demanding styles and grammar might also have encouraged the listener to stick with him in the more difficult parts, to trust him to provide "compensation" for the effort required to make it through the work. In any case, the acclaim which followed the première, at least for the more general listener, would not have been rooted in the more abstract theoretical issues; nor would the general public have many among them who could hear the subtle transformation of musical figures which molds the contrasting movements into a coherent whole.[1]

Given the success of the individual movements, it is tempting to stop at this point, and to accept the suite as a series of well-made tone poems. However, Holst's intention for the work to be taken as a single structure demands a deeper look at both his large-scale structural techniques and his use of idiom and compositional devices.

The mixture of musical idioms

Overall, there is a general preference for mixing idioms in the individual movements, in spite of the composer's claim for a lack of contrast within movements. The paradox is only apparent and is unravelled by an understanding of the means by which he employed variety to enrich a single character. The subtitles encouraged listeners to interpret all that they heard in each movement within a single metaphor. At the same time, he seems to have made sure that, within the various idioms and styles used, the main metaphoric gesture or style could still be discerned.

In *Mars* the battle metaphor is always present, but in various guises. The opening $\frac{5}{4}$ rhythmic figure, while not specifically "military," is easily heard as such through its percussive and repetitive aspects; and in the second half of the movement the figure is taken up by the snare drum to reinforce the metaphor. But $\frac{5}{4}$ was something of a "cutting-edge" meter at the time, seldom used (though Holst himself was fond of it) and not easily assimilated. It is clearly contrasted by the more accurate military-march style of the third theme at mm. 80–3. There is a marching-band sound about the melodic line and the harmony here, not to mention the woodwind- and brass-dominated orchestration. While the meter is still $\frac{5}{4}$, it does not intrude on the rhythmic sense of the melody. The other tonal passage in *Mars*, the A♭ section at mm. 25–8, is *nobilmente* in character and could assume the popular military style exemplified by Elgar's *Pomp and Circumstance* marches. The contrast serves to heighten the severity of the rest of the movement and its lack of common-practice grammar. *Mars*, then, is almost totally avant-garde in its language, unlike the battle music of *Ein Heldenleben* which is clearly rooted in nineteenth-century practice. Holst uses the contrasting marching-band style to highlight the character of the new language as appropriately alien in its effect.

Venus, in contrast, is rooted in nineteenth-century harmonic and melodic practice. Within this, however, is a subtle but clear use of the slower harmonic rhythm and easy melodic principles of popular music, particularly of the Edwardian "shop ballad." This movement was sometimes cited as one of the weaker movements of the suite, perhaps because of this sentimental style. Holst's use of the style is enriched by harmonic surprise at crucial places – for instance the resolution to a mediant chord at m. 34, where the move from the subdominant to a tonic chord would be closer to the sentimental style. Likewise, the plaintive gesture at m. 68, resolving into the sweetly chromatic G half-diminished chord, is "saved" by the ensuing truly chromatic surprise, F♯ major (Ex. 4.6).

The other movements have their own combinations of styles. A Straussian humor pervades *Mercury*, and, while it tends to be insecure in its tonal bearings, it clearly partakes of the nineteenth century. On the other hand, the trio theme must have been heard as somewhat exotic and perhaps vaguely "Eastern." Holst's particular "topic" for this melodic/harmonic style – a short repeating melodic phrase with an open-ended harmonic progression – was firmly established in *Beni Mora* (1909–10), subtitled *Oriental Suite for*

Orchestra. As for *Jupiter*, the *pesante* theme is a dance of the music-hall variety, though it has a certain popular-folk quality, as does the Mixolydian tune in $\frac{3}{4}$ which follows it. These are contrasted with the hymn style of the center theme, which was called, in Eric Blom's Queen's Hall program notes, "a kind of exalted folksong." The opening syncopated theme is a true hybrid, somewhat suggestive of a Gilbert and Sullivan patter, though the orchestration gives it greater weight and legitimacy. *Uranus* is also filled with hybrids: vaudevillian gestures and military marches subsumed by a general parody treatment reminiscent of *Till Eulenspiegel*.

Saturn and *Neptune* are stylistically the most pure in treatment, though both make use of stylistic suggestion. *Saturn*'s B minor processional theme moves folklike around the Dorian mode combination of flattened 7th and raised 6th scale degrees. What is most often recalled in *Neptune* is the avant-garde *Klangfarben* texture, with its dissonant sonorities; yet it also has a touch of the Dorian mode in the clarinet theme (mm. 58 ff). Ironically, the final chord in both *Neptune* and *Venus* (major with added 6th) so closely associated now with a sentimental ballad style, was not found in popular music at the time, and actually was, for the British audience, more modern as a closing chord than present listeners might imagine.

Some gestures found throughout the various movements have since been recognized as part of Holst's personal style. The preference for $\frac{5}{4}$ meter is one example; the use of polychords another. More specific to the composer are his compositional processes: the use of ostinato, the mosaic-like connection of melodic fragments, and the lack of Beethovenian-style development. There is also a particular set of contrasts which Holst was to use throughout his career, such as simple triads versus more dissonant structures, and the use of traditional melody versus a more fragmented style.[2] Through all of this there seems to be an emphasis on contrast and disjunctive combination which should lead to a sense of pastiche, at best; at worst it should lead to incoherence. What holds all together is the consistency of the Holstian treatment. Every movement uses the same musical processes in some way: the mixture of idioms, the enriching contrasts of musical character. More subtle, but also more significant, is that all of the material is controlled by the composer's economy and precision. Every note of melody and harmony is essential; there is no decoration or padding. Every use of repetition is tied either to a growth process in harmonization or orchestration, or to the needs of the character – the relentlessness of *Mars*, the folkiness of *Jupiter*, the timelessness of *Neptune*. Furthermore, most of his figures "reduce" to very basic shapes – perfect 5th up, minor 2nd down; five-note lower neighbor

Ex. 6.1   *Jupiter*, center theme

figure – so that figures in later movements are actually developments of earlier ones.

Holst's sense of economy and precision can be exemplified through an analysis of the center theme in *Jupiter*. It appears to be straightforward enough, without decorative pitches and little contrapuntal elaboration (see Ex. 6.1).

To begin with, the melody is built primarily from only two figures, bracketed as "a" and (in the reduction line) "b" in Example 6.1. These figures account for almost all the notes; the remainder are important for adding motivation and balance to the line. The main figures are simple and can be found as the material of many English folksongs. The melody unfolds in very small increments, first the figure "a," then figure "c" followed by an "a" with a larger opening leap. In comparing the two "a" figures it can be seen that the rhythm of the second connects the E♭ repeating on beats 1 and 2. In retrospect, the first "a" also has a repeating pitch at its finish, though the initial analysis did not include it. This repeated-note motive recurs to end the phrase, strengthening its importance and allowing the repeat of "a" at the beginning of the second phrase to be extended one beat. Furthermore, to begin the second phrase with the "a" figure "makes sense" because the first phrase ended with the reverse of "a." The arching form of this first phrase together with its tendency toward C minor rather than the more predictable E♭ major set up an expectation in the listener to start over again – which is exactly what happens.

The second phrase, using the same figures, serves as a consequent phrase. It moves to the anticipated key of E♭ through the slightest of variation: the repeated note is put off to the end of the phrase's third measure. This small change is significant, accomplishing two ends: it recalls the "laughing" figure from mm. 47–8; and it forces the line to arch higher, and subsequently to close at the higher pitch of tonic E♭. This seems to be of far more consequence than the few pitches could effect, especially since there is so much repeated from the beginning; yet any alteration from Holst's structure either diminishes the strength of effect or sabotages it completely.

The second half of the theme evolves from the first half: palindromic "a" figures flanking a "b" structure (Ex. 6.1, reduction line). While the first half leisurely unfolded the underlying "b," the final measures of the theme present a compressed version, gaining momentum toward the next full statement. Midway through the second half, the original "a" (G–B♭–C) appears, an octave higher than at first, creating a spiralling effect. In fact, the whole line centers around the treble clef B♭, a 5th above the focus of the first half of the theme; and it ends without a terminating cadence, thus serving as a launching pad for its restatement in the next octave. Continuance and intensification is therefore secured without sounding contrived. On the third and final go-round one begins to wonder how the melody achieved such height, emotively or registrally. The apparent simplicity of materials and technique is truly deceptive. The development of this melody is as natural as a folksong, while being rhetorically much stronger.

And it is this development process which ultimately leads the listener through the musical – and metaphoric – plot.

The first plot: the transformation of the first theme of *Mars*

Until this point the analytical descriptions have centered on individual movements. This approach highlighted the interaction of the various movements: mood pictures which act as foils for one another. Yet there is an appropriateness to the order of movements and an emotive and aesthetic momentum which builds as the work proceeds, and which needs further explanation. Holst appears to have established this emotive and metaphoric progression by using a set of developmental "plots" which carry individual musical figures from one movement to the next. At the local, and most obvious, level for the listener, the main musical plot of the work is found in the development of the opening melodic figure of *Mars*. The briefest summary of the action is this: "the gradual re-orientation and stabilization of the downward moving minor 2nd." The introduction of this interval as a tonal dissonance at the beginning of *Mars* is finally resolved as a stable cadence figure at the close of the last movement of the piece. There are obviously other character issues to be dealt with, particularly the problem of stabilizing polychords and key fusion, and the "training" of the listener to hear an alternative tonality. But the motivation for the listener to continue working through the piece is in the gestural action. The outline of this prime musical action is given as Example 6.2.

The first event involving the main figure, given against the opening ostinato, is the development of the three-note motive described in Chapter 4 (Ex. 6.2*a–c*). The shift at m. 25 into the tonal area of Ab brings about a change in the basic gesture: the minor 2nd is replaced by the major 2nd (Ex. 6.2*c*). The new interval is both less tense and more tonal, for it establishes a conventional major scale. So when the phrase ends in m. 29 out of key (B[Cb] = Ab: b3) it is a shock.

Over the next ten measures the repeated efforts of the cadential figure heard at m. 29 to close simply reinforce the dissonance of the gesture. When, in m. 40, the pedal G progresses to C, the B does move up as well, but the *essential* minor 2nd (involving a downward close, Db to C) does not occur. The result is Db against C (Ex. 6.2*d*), the most dissonant and physically aggressive form of the interval yet encountered.[3] Several further versions of the opening interval set (perfect 5th, minor 2nd, [tritone]) occur in the succeeding themes of the movement, as seen in Example 6.2*e, g*. These are from the second and third themes, respectively. Both of these maintain the dissonant and, by now, unyielding aspect of the character, and Example 6.2*g* cross-references the military/war metaphor through its fanfare nature. Interestingly enough, it is in this form that a Db–C *resolution* is first heard, in mm. 142–3 in the tenor tuba, but the move and its sense of resolution, are obscured by the Ab chord which occurs simultaneously as the second-theme gesture interrupts the action. It is not until the final cadence of the movement (mm. 184–5, Ex. 6.2*h*) that the interval set resolves; and here it disappears rather than resolves, as no Db actually moves to C.

While the succeeding movements are occupied primarily with the development of their own characters, elements of the main plot do occur, thus allowing each to contribute to the main musical action. In *Venus* this occurs in mm. 15–16 (Ex. 6–2*i*). At this point, the bass line and harmony produce an upper leading-tone cadence, Ab: bII–I, the first full cadence of the movement. The oscillating F and Eb, at the top of the texture, are synonymous of the Db–B oscillation of the first major cadential attempt in *Mars* (mm. 28–9 ff).

73

Ex. 6.2   Plotting the transformation of the first theme of *Mars*

Ex. 6.2   (continued)

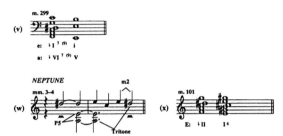

At the same time the Eb works with the bass Bʰ to form the characteristic tritone, and with the bass Ab to complete the restoration of stability in the perfect 5th.

There are other gestures in *Venus* which continue to work toward the resolution of the *Mars* figure. The most prominent is at mm. 46ff (Ex. 6.2*j*), appearing again at m. 70 and m. 106. In this figure, the interval set is reorientated in another tonal context, this time utilizing the rhythm and linear nature of the original.

The most obvious contribution to this plot found in *Mercury* is first heard in mm. 1–4 and carries on throughout the outer sections of the movement (Ex. 6.2*k*). The chord roots Bb and E are synonymic with the G–Db of *Mars*, though in *Mercury* the semitone opens the tritone and achieves tonic closure – a reversal, and balancing, of the initial point of tension as found in the first movement. The second contribution is found abstracted from mm. 70–3 (Ex. 6.2*l*) in which the perfect 5th to minor 2nd move of the opening figure of *Mars* is enlarged upon.

It is in *Saturn* that the initial figure resurfaces in a clearly recognizable form. In mm. 4–6 ff (Ex. 6.2*m*), the tritone is prominent, but the aggressive bite is replaced with a more sedate aspect. This is brought about through two points: the use of a *static* B half-diminished chord to undergird the passage, and the *resolution* down by minor 2nd in the melody to the note B. Both points suggest this note as a tonal center, even if not as a functional tonic. It is strange to think of a tritone chord as stable; however, the absence of tonal functional movement and the quiet instrumentation both modify the psychological effect of the theoretically dissonant sonority. If the central problem of the suite is to find a way to justify the initial dissonance without denying its nature, then the opening of *Saturn* provides the first look at a solution framed in Holst's musical language.

The succeeding elements which *Saturn* contributes to this plot serve to modify its own initial element into a more traditional tonal form (Ex. 6.2*n–p*). The oscillating major 2nd of *Saturn* ties it clearly to *Venus* and the two characters are also linked through the manner with which each deals with the initial plot element, transforming it into an acceptable tonal gesture. *Uranus*, on the other hand, reasserts the aspect of tonal dissonance, as seen in Example 6.2*q* (mm. 9–11 ff). This movement is generally considered a scherzo, but within that context there is still a march to be heard, linking it with *Mars*. The suite seems to have come full circle, or, since this movement is more tonal than *Mars* in its grammar, in a spiral. The theme represented in Example 6.2*q* combines motives from themes 1 and 2 of *Mars* in a less destabilizing, non-threatening, even humorous, form (see Chapter 5). Other elements recall gestural relations from other movements while developing the initial *Mars* figure. Particularly, the theme at m. 46 (Ex. 6.2*r*) parodies the B minor theme in *Saturn* (Ex. 6.2*n*), while the figure at m. 50 (Ex. 6.2*s*) parodies mm. 68–9 in *Venus*. The final contribution of *Uranus*, though, is not a parody, but a close parallel to the ♭2–1 cadence in *Venus* (Ex. 6.2*i*): a true ♭II–I progression (Ex. 6.2*v*). It is (metaphorically) marred by the origin of the penultimate chord: coming from the key of C, the F7(9) sounds clearly subdominant, while the use of the note E against it (mm. 241–6) orientates it slightly toward the key of A (F7 = A: augmented 6th). The use of D♯ and the resolution of the F–D♯ interval outward to octave E's is also consistent with this analysis. So the final move is ambiguous.

(chords)		C	–	F9	–	E
(key/functions)	C:	I		IV		
	e:			♭II	–	i

The ♭2–1 which closes *Mars* has finally been given a functional context, but it is not yet secure. The link from C major is strong enough to weaken the sense of finality, for there has not been enough evidence of E minor to overcome the long C major section which preceded this ending. Also, the final E–B is so faint and so low in register that it is virtually not heard. This, of course, establishes the need for a last movement, *Neptune* to create the true final cadence.

Neptune, appropriately, contributes to the plot only indirectly, by suggesting the relevant themes of other movements (see "The second plot," below); there is, however, a tritone–semitone set heard early on (Ex. 6.2*w*). Most significant, though, is the reuse of the final cadence of *Uranus* as the final cadence for the entire piece (Ex. 6.2*x*). In this final presentation the F7(9) chord is better prepared, the prevailing tonality of E having been firmly established at least seventeen measures before the cadence. Furthermore, the C minor chord formed by the upper partials of the F7(9) is clearly identified in relation to E through its resolution to C♯ minor with the notes E–B following closely in the bass (m. 85). By first presenting the F–E gesture against the note B, as the dominant note of E, the function of the F chord as E: ♭II is clearly reinterpreted as a substitute for the dominant chord.

This main musical action, as has been described here, is an articulation over time of a single gesture and its variants; it also indicates the presence of a network of variations which comes to bear on the development of the central interval set. At the same time, the larger structure articulates the development of key/character correlations and motivates the movement from the "physical" key of C to the "mystical" key of E.

The second plot: the search for large-scale structural control

It is clear from a study of the key reduction of the suite (Ex. 6.3) that each movement operates within a traditional dominant–tonic polarity. In some movements the progression does not start on the tonic but resolves to it, for example *Mars* and *Saturn*. *Venus* is a special case, in which the opening key area of E♭ (implied) – serving as a structural dominant and progressing (via III) to its conventional tonic – also ends the movement. This forms a double hierarchy, focusing on A♭ (as the stable key of both exposition and recapitulation), and alternatively on E♭ (as the implied opening key and the stable closing key). Another, somewhat different, sort of double hierarchy is found in *Saturn*. In this case the opening harmonic entity (B) serves as a leading-tone chord to one tonic (C) and as an altered dominant to the other (E). The B also serves as a conventional tonal region for the theme I*b* (mm. 30ff), focusing attention on the E–B polarity. However, the area of C is also prominent, as tonic of the second theme, and it is the prime tonic at the close.

These double hierarchies are tangled by virtue of the ambiguity of tonal focus at the beginning of most movements. *Mars* has too little information to establish a tonic systematically; *Venus* uses implied tonics with no tonic chord present; *Mercury* passes quickly over its tonic and never properly resolves, forcing the listener to accept a new harmonic logic. Other movements have similar ambiguities: *Saturn* has already been mentioned in this regard. *Jupiter*, while establishing its tonic early, does not do it convincingly and settles into the supertonic for its first theme, resolving finally to tonic at the point of recapitulation. The tangled perspective is apparently an important aspect of

Ex. 6.3   Key scheme for *The Planets*

the language, and Holst establishes the concept at the beginning of *Mars* at the most local level. But its greatest significance is its effect on the key relations among movements (Ex. 6.3). These form a symmetrical "matrix" built around an augmented chord and its dominants.

dominants:	D♯ (E♭)	–	G	–	B
tonics:	G♯ (A♭)	–	C	–	E

or

G♯ (A♭)	D♯
	⟩ m2
E	B
	⟩ m2
C	G
	⟩ m2
	A♭ (G♯)

The matrix can also be manipulated to form three major–minor chords, the main structure of the *Klangfarben* section of *Neptune*:

A♭ major–minor:	A♭	–	C♭	–	C	–	E♭
E major–minor:	E	–	G	–	G♯	–	B
C major–minor:	C	–	E♭	–	E	–	G

This matrix is more a structural control than a rhetorical force, and local function moves away from the traditional conventions only gradually. At the local level most progression to tonic is achieved through dominant or leading-tone harmonies. This is true also of the alternative logic: ♭II7 is ♭2–4–♭6–♭1 (♯7); root motion by major third is ♭6–♭1(♯7)–3 resolving to 5–1–3. An alternative to this functional motion is the use of bi-modal chords (major–minor chords) progressing to straight triads, as found in *Neptune*. Yet even here, it is the lower third which disappears in the resolution, so it acts as a leading tone giving way to the structurally stronger note a half-step above it.

Root motion by major 3rd also controls the choice of key for individual movements and establishes a large-scale musical action between *Mars*, as the opening, and *Neptune*: the completion of the augmented triad C–E–G♯. The use of keys throughout the suite promotes the idea of a search for this symmetrical structure. For example, *Mars* ends on C, but it takes the entire

Ex. 6.4   *Neptune*, m. 1

movement, beginning ambiguously in G, to find it. The D–D♭ gesture of the opening is completed at the end by having D♭ give way to C. This not only reproduces the opening minor 2nd (half-step) move as a closing figure, it also reorientates the line from G:5–♮4 to C:2–♭2–1. The final tonic is not *functionally* secure, however; only the relaxation of the tension between components of the D♭/C polychord hints at the sense of key. The search in *Venus* is similar. The first stable key, A♭, is reached only after a movement through the A♭ minor triad: E♭–C♭–A♭. The recapitulatory return to A♭ is redirected, reversing the route through the triad, so the key is "lost" at the end. *Mercury* follows a pattern that is much the same: ambiguity partially cleared, and an ultimate losing of the apparently most appropriate tonal center.

But as the listener works through the suite the keys which continue to be highlighted are C, E, and G♯, and their traditional dominants. At the end of *Jupiter*, the sudden digression from C major to G♯ minor (B major) emphasizes the distance between components of the augmented triad, but it also focuses on what is to come. *Saturn* is a direct consequence of this glimpse into the future, for it is here that both the main musical action (Plot I) and the search for the tonal matrix begins in earnest. This movement establishes the connection between C and E. *Uranus*, in its last theme, connects all three, C and E and G♯; and *Neptune* begins by demonstrating the half-step, contrary motion voice-leading which creates the alternative tonal grammar (Ex. 6.4). Thus the suite can be perceived as a search for a symmetrical tonal matrix – G♯ (and D♯ or E♭), C (and G), E (and B) – as both a controlling structure and a product of alternative tonal principles.

It was shown in Chapter 5 that the figure in Example 6.4 was rooted in a traditional tonal dynamic. The sonorities which follow in the *farben* section are developments of the figure, moving the listener away from tonal function toward the alternative function and its symmetrical key matrix of G♯–C–E. At mm. 85–91 the final harmonic structure is achieved: E major (with added 6th) coming out of C minor.

At m. 100, the complete cadence formula, first heard at the end of *Uranus*, is heard resolving to the E6. The C minor chord is subsumed as the upper components of a dominant function in E (F9 over B) (mm. 94 ff) and its darkness is dispelled by the brighter V–I (♭II/5–I) progression. Then the dominant note itself is let loose (m. 100), allowing the remaining ♭II9–I6 cadence to echo, literally, into the distance. The last measures are a summing up of previous issues:

- The resolution of the oscillating half-diminished chords to E major 6th (C♯ minor 7th) in *Saturn*, m. 105;

- The ♭II–I6 resolution in *Venus*, mm. 15–16;

- The C minor of *Mars* (sublimated into the F chord in *Uranus*) resolves to the 'peaceful' major 6th chord first heard in *Venus*;

- The sublimating F chord in *Uranus*, m. 222, resolving to E;

- The alternative voice-leading principle: contrary motion half steps.

Thus *Neptune* becomes the locus of arrival, of resolution – the end of the search for structural first principles. *Jupiter* was often used as a closing movement in partial performances because of its rhetorical strength; its combination of celebration and noble sentiment gave almost any grouping of movements a fitting close. In the full suite this movement acts as a slingshot, its festive nature and easy tonality flinging the listener into the further reaches of the outer planets. It is only with *Neptune* that we arrive at the point where the metaphor of mystical serenity is joined to the fact of musical resolution.

The third plot: musical character and the search for serenity

This plot is a conceptual one, affording not an action (in either the musical or the literary sense) but an experiential argument. Each movement projects a single character moving, by name, deliberately from physical aggression and ambition (*Mars*) to metaphysical and mystical serenity (*Neptune*). The move is not a simple one, metaphorically or systematically. The composer provides the sense of a radical breach of the traditional tonal system; metaphorically, of the empirical foundations of the (tonal) world. At the same time, he calls for an acceptance of an only dimly understood subjective world view: a "new" tonal logic. And it requires the qualities of art (Venus), flexibility (Mercury), perseverance (Saturn), and reckless eccentricity (Uranus) to move from the obvious attempt at reconciliation (Jupiter) to the detachment of stoicism

(Neptune). As a system, this becomes an argument for the subversion of traditional tonal function. But it is a subversion from within, the seeds of destruction sown in both war and peace, both *Mars* and *Venus*. Ultimately, the entire structure moves from traditional tonal assumptions – worked out in the first four movements – to a set of alternative functional concepts which gradually emerge in the second half of the piece.

The move from physical aggression to mystical serenity is achieved through musical action on several levels. There is a correlation of key with character: C (minor or major) with physical qualities; A♭ (G♯) and E♭ with stability and self-content; and E with the final metaphysical and mystical state. This is matched by a set of characteristic functional systems: conventional tonality, extended tonality (highlighting ♭II and other polymodal functions), and the apparently non-functional alternations culminating in *Neptune*. These are not aligned with particular keys in any strict way, but are combined to create more subtle variations in character. Also, the various gestural plots propel characteristic gestures of earlier movements through the musical actions of each later one. The gestures are meant to be heard as self-contained musical entities; and as such they function as metaphors in the program. For instance, the pounding, non-resolving semitone dissonance of *Mars* embodies aggressiveness and the sense of ordeal, while the functionally resolving semitones of *Venus* are acquiescent and pacific.

The musical actions which bring about such metaphorical change were described in the narration of the first plot, above. These local actions are sometimes the agents of their own development, as is the case with the opening theme of *Mars*, in which the D–D♭ semitone slip creates enough dissonance to push itself forward in search of resolution. At other times the source of developmental energy is wrought through a change in idiom, as happens with the more sentimental style in *Venus*. The semitone there is put in a functional context, albeit one "on the edge." A change of idiom is also at work in *Saturn*, when the opening impressionistic haze is followed by the B minor version of the theme in a folklike Dorian mode setting. Finally, the force of extramusical association, as in *Uranus*, can promulgate a change in musical character. The unexpected combination of disparate stylistic suggestions in the opening creates a sense of wit which allows parody to take place. When the opening tritone–semitone figure is subjected to this new, and somewhat ridiculous, functional context the musical character undergoes radical transformation. Holst's own persona, created by the masterful orchestration and the deft handling of musical figures, also contributes to the developmental process.

81

There is a sense of authority and of intelligence beyond the grasp of the listener, as each movement goes further beyond the horizon of musical expectation.

Musical character versus programmaticism

The narrative element as described here must be understood to exist within a very specific rhetorical convention – the same which surrounded Beethoven's Sixth Symphony, for example, but different from the programmaticism of *Till Eulenspiegel*. Holst's insistence on the lack of a program in *The Planets*, while admitting the term "mood picture," will not, using this distinction, be inconsistent. The programmaticism to which Holst refers is a literary one, which was popularized not only by Richard Strauss, but also by such works as Tchaikovsky's *1812 Overture* and even Beethoven's *Wellington's Victory*, not to mention the works of Holst's British contemporary, Josef Holbrooke. While Holst might not have been swayed by these lesser works, the ballet music of Stravinsky would have been extremely potent. But these all tell stories. The model for Holst's work would be found in Debussy's *Images*, Delius's tone poems (just beginning to be heard in London in 1907) and Elgar's *Enigma Variations*. The evocative potential of Wagner's music, *as music rather than narrative*, is also not to be discounted.

The term "plot" in these pages, then, is used with the assumption that there is no reference to literary narrative. No other word seems to convey the forward motion and progressive effect which pulls both musical and metaphoric actions together. Furthermore, the term connotes – and this is true in literary theory as well – a *motivated* series of events. The plots described here are not literary stories, nor specific dramas; they are, however, highly motivated musical actions. This brings the discussion back to the principles of metaphor in music with which this book began, for the musical plot is the vehicle for the psychological development which listeners perceive as unfolding before them. The listening conventions developed in tandem with European art-music empowered music to serve as a projection of the real world, going beyond mere symbolism to true experience.

And this is the strongest possible explanation for the staying power of *The Planets*. The characters are palpable because the musical process is both systematic and consistently *human*. Like all great music, the materials, taken separately, may become dated, but the manner in which musical events are articulated continues to move a willing audience.

Epilogue

Outside of the chapter in Bernard Shore's *Sixteen Symphonies* and the one chapter in Imogen Holst's *The Music of Gustav Holst*, there was no detailed analytical work done concerning *The Planets* until the recent publication of Michael Short's book on the composer.[1] Most studies of Holst's music in recent years have focused on vocal works such as *The Hymn of Jesus* and his late instrumental works, especially *Egdon Heath* and *Hammersmith*; yet popular interest in the suite has not diminished. There are nearly two dozen recordings currently available, and several historic performances, including Holst's acoustic recording from 1926, have now been released. The apparent lack of critical interest over the last sixty years needs to be explored in the face of the suite's popular success and influence.

Once the complexity of the language used in *The Planets* is understood, it becomes difficult to explain its appeal to the larger audience as being due to an assumed superficiality of content; yet such is the stigma of programmaticism that it diverts attention from the essential value of the work. In the case of Holst's suite, the intensity of character in each movement frequently overwhelmed the reviewers' larger critical awareness, so that descriptions of the composition were nearly always steeped in metaphor and melopoietic allusion, with little technical or theoretical discussion. It was also this intensity which must have swept up the general audience – who were, perhaps, totally unaware of the various musical, literary, pictorial, mythological, and even astrological references bandied about by critics – for no other classical music would have had for them the combination of power, novelty, and clarity of image displayed by the individual movements. Sir Adrian Boult's comment about the moment-to-moment way of listening which characterized the general public's approach to music is to be remembered here. Holst's strategy of maintaining a single strong character for each *Planet* and his ability to build musical structures which acted as true metaphors of character capitalize on this listening convention. At the same time, however, the sophisticated use of such novel devices as juxtaposed meters, chordal counterpoint, and bitonality made it extremely difficult to assimilate the work as a formal and grammatical object.

That is to say, the very things which made the suite intense and novel, and thus popular, obscured the true theoretical significance of the composition. Furthermore, since Holst himself had gone on, by this time, to even more distended tonal and formal concepts, critics either overlooked *The Planets* as an early work or as merely developmental, or they began to discount the composer's efforts completely. For those who must have known the work intimately (L. Dunton Green, Richard Capell, and Sir Donald Tovey) the composition seems to have suffered a similar fate. Tovey was more taken with the power of *The Hymn of Jesus* and *The Perfect Fool*, the texts of which gave Holst's novel constructions more scope as melopoietic support. Capell, as mentioned in Chapter 2, went so far as to secure inclusion for the suite in Bernard Shore's book, *Sixteen Symphonies*; yet Shore's use of Capell's earlier article on the work demonstrates both his own lack of interest and his friend's conventional and theoretically unilluminating approach. In this case, the original article, like Imogen Holst's description, follows the "analytical program note" format established by Tovey early in the century, diluted to address a general readership. Such an approach was expected in the popular press and "culture" periodicals; however, even the more serious venues avoided theoretical discussions, most likely because there was no ready context in which to place them.

In Holst's day, theoretical discussions were based on one of two ideas: the conservative, prescriptive principles of classical oratory, or the progressive metaphor of organic growth. The working method embodied in *The Planets* does not lend itself to either context. However, over the last ten to fifteen years there has been an increased interest in music as an expressive rhetorical experience, i.e. music as a generic form of communication. There have been a number of books and articles dealing with the issue of "sub-texts" in music. The plot-symphony ideal found in Beethoven's Fifth, Sixth and Ninth Symphonies and the suppressed programs of Mahler's symphonies are two good examples of this area of interest. There has also been a rising interest in the musico–literary cross-references of the Symbolist movement and Wagner's music-drama ideal. These recent efforts provide an ample context for renewed discussions regarding *The Planets*, for in this milieu the correlation of musical grammar and gesture with human experience is the essential task. The biological metaphor of music as a self-generating system is replaced with the *convention* of music as a self-enclosed universe which is empowered as a metaphor for human existence. In this light Holst's suite becomes a highly compelling model which should not be overlooked.

For Holst himself, the work supplied a practical example for his future tonal language which was to be built from its alternative tonal principles and bi-modal and bi-chordal entities. Holst was to formulate new scales from these novel combinations to develop a true extended tonal system. Likewise, the polychords of *Saturn* and *Neptune* were to lead to what Edmund Rubbra called "key fusions," a "complex-tonality" which allowed for a highly expressive use of tonic "quality." This is a rhetoric, rather than a grammar, of tonality.[2] Holst also found ways to subvert traditional tonal grammar, i.e. the principles which, as in the verbal arts, allow a listener to develop a manageable universe for future artistic events. In the second theme of *Mars*, the chordal parallelisms violate the conventional general principles involving intervals (for example perfect 5th must not be followed by another perfect 5th). The effect is much like using a string of only nouns or only verbs in a sentence: there is no grammar to create sense. In the case of music, the parallelisms work against tonal sense. The device forces the listener to focus on the musical material as gesture, rather than as grammar, thus adding to the expressive and imaging power of the passage. Holst returns to this device in his later orchestral works, both as alternative (non)-grammar and as a stylistic icon.

Perhaps the most significant use of *The Planets* as a model for Holst is his adaptation of the B minor theme of *Saturn* as his "old man" processional theme in *Egdon Heath*. Here it is demonstrated that Holst's musical journey was not merely a technical one. Like the suite, the composer was on a psychological expedition, one which lasted for the rest of his life, and is exemplified by his later compositions. "In *Neptune*," says Bernard Shore in closing his essay, "Holst leaves his friends and, unguided, sets forth into the unknown by himself – and none sees him return." Clearly, he did not return, in his later works, to the extraordinary popularity and appeal of *The Planets*, yet the work serves as a guide for those who choose to follow. In this regard we can apply to Holst what was said of one of his favorite composers, Haydn:

his music enters our ears quite smoothly, for we have a sense that we are hearing something that is easily perceived and already familiar to us; but we soon find it is not that which we had thought it was or which we thought it should become. We hear something new and are amazed at the master, who knew so cunningly how to offer us, under the guise of the well known, something never before heard.[3]

Appendix 1

Holst's public performances, 1908–21

The following lists are collated from the reviews and programs in the Holst Press Cuttings Collection, held at The Holst Birthplace Museum, Cheltenham. It is as complete a picture as can be obtained of performances of Holst's works. However, the lists do not include the many performances of songs at solo and joint recitals, nor do they include school-sponsored performances. Furthermore, it is not to be expected that reviews from outside Great Britain would have always reached the composer, nor that all performances would be reviewed. Therefore, the lists should be considered a good, though incomplete, representation of his public performance history.

Table 1: List of Holst's public performances, 1908–14

1908		
16 Jan.	India	*Two Songs Without Words* (orch)
4 April	London	*King Estmere* (ch/orch)
19 Dec.	London	*3 Folk Songs* (ch/orch) (from *7 Folk Songs*, M78)
1909		
11 Dec.	London	*Songs of the West* (rev) (orch)
1910		
6 April	London	*A Somerset Rhapsody* (orch)
24 June	London	*A Somerset Rhapsody*
19 Oct.	Birmingham	*A Somerset Rhapsody*
17 Nov.	Bath	*Songs of the West*
		A Somerset Rhapsody
1911		
16 March	Blackpool	*Choral Hymns from the Rig Veda III*
22 March	London	*Choral Hymns from the Rig Veda II*
28 April	London	*Four Vedic Hymns*, op. 24
2 May	London	*A Somerset Rhapsody*
2 May	London	*Invocation* (ch/orch)
May?	London	*Suite no. 2 for Military Band*
31 Oct.	Lincoln	*A Somerset Rhapsody*
Nov.	Bournemouth	*A Somerset Rhapsody*

Table 1 (*cont.*)

22 Nov.	London	*Two Vedic Hymns*, op. 24
6 Dec.	Newcastle	*Choral Hymns from the Rig Veda I*
18 Dec.	London	*Four Old English Carols*

1912

11 Jan.	Bournemouth	*A Somerset Rhapsody*
18 Jan.	Manchester	*A Somerset Rhapsody*
21 March	Blackpool	*Two Eastern Pictures* (ch)
25 March	London	*Choral Hymns from the Rig Veda I*
1 May	London	*Beni Mora* (orch)
29 May	Paris	*Choral Hymns from the Rig Veda I*
23 July	London	*Phantastes Suite* (orch)
15 Oct.	London	*Marching Song* (from *Two Songs Without Words*)
24 Oct.	Newcastle	*Beni Mora*
12 Nov.	London	*Beautiful Nancy* (v/p)
17 Dec.	Newcastle	*Choral Hymns from the Rig Veda I*

1913

3 Jan.	Birmingham	*Beni Mora*
11 Feb.	London	*Two Eastern Pictures*
25 Feb.	London	*The Mystic Trumpeter* (v/orch)
27 Feb.	London	*Choral Hymns from the Rig Veda III*
4 March	London	*The Cloud Messenger* (ch/orch)
7 March	London	*Choral Hymns from the Rig Veda III*/1, 3
10 March	Blackburn	*Two Eastern Pictures*
		Choral Hymns from the Rig Veda III
		Songs from *The Princess*
13 March	Leicester	*Choral Hymns from the Rig Veda III*
26 March	Edinburgh	*Choral Hymns from the Rig Veda I*
?	Stratford	*Two Songs Without Words* (used by RVW during the Shakespeare festival)
8 Nov.	London	*Marching Song* (from *Two Songs Without Words*)
17 Nov.	London	*A Somerset Rhapsody*
20 Nov.	London	*Beni Mora*/3
15 Dec.	Birmingham	*Beni Mora*
16 Dec.	London	*Four Old English Carols*

1914

15 Jan.	Manchester	*Beni Mora*
3 Feb.	Leicester	*Choral Hymns from the Rig Veda I, II*
10 March	London	*Hymn to Dionysus* (fch/orch)
18 March	London	*Choral Hymns from the Rig Veda IV*
6 May	Morecambe	*The Homecoming* (ch)
13 May	Birmingham	*Choral Hymns from the Rig Veda III*
19 May	Birmingham	*Choral Hymns from the Rig Veda III*
10 July	London	*Carnival* from *Suite de Ballet* (orch)

Table 2: List of Holst's public performances, 1915–21

1915

| 17 Nov. | Lincoln | *Two Songs Without Words* |

1916

Spring	Newcastle	*The Cloud Messenger*
		Choral Hymns from the Rig Veda III
5 Dec.	London	*Savitri* (op)
19 Dec.	London	*Terly Terlow* (ch)
		Lullay My Liking (ch)

1917

12 March	Newcastle	*Choral Hymns from the Rig Veda II*
		Tears' Idle Tears (ch)
		Pastoral (ch)
		Ave Maria (ch)
13 March	London	*Invocation*
29 Nov.	London	*Phantasy on British Folksongs* (str q)
15 Dec.	Newcastle	*Of One That Is So Fair and Bright* (ch)

1918

4 Feb.	London	*Country Song* (from *Two Songs Without Words*)
18 March	London	*Vedic Hymns*
4 April	London	*Four Songs for Voice and Violin*
16 April	London	*Three Choral Folksongs* (3 of 6)
4 May	London	*Four Songs for Voice and Violin*
27 June	Manchester	*Two Songs Without Words*
29 Sep.	London	THE PLANETS (private performance)

[Holst off to Salonika]

1919

27 Feb.	London	THE PLANETS (M, Me, J, S, U)
19 March	Newcastle	*Hymn to Dionysus* (ch)
22 March	Brighton	*Japanese Suite* (orch)

[Holst back in England]

4 July	London	*Two Songs Without Words*
		Carnival (from *Suite de Ballet*)
1 Sep.	London	*Japanese Suite*
19 Oct.	London	*Japanese Suite*
22 Nov.	London	THE PLANETS (V, M, J)
14 Dec.	London	THE PLANETS (V, M, J)
23 Dec.	London	*This Have I Done for My True Love* (ch)

1920

| 29 Jan. | London | *Beni Mora* |
| 25 March | London | *The Hymn of Jesus* (ch/orch) |

Table 2 (*cont.*)

2 June	London	*The Hymn of Jesus*
13 June	Oxford	*The Hymn of Jesus*
Summer	London	*The Hymn of Jesus*
18 July	Newcastle	*Two Psalms* (ch/orch)
19 Sep.	Birmingham	*Japanese Suite*
		Jig (from *St. Paul's Suite*)
		The Djinn (from *The Sneezing Charm*)
10 Oct.	Birmingham	THE PLANETS (M, V, Me, S, J)
15 Nov.	London	THE PLANETS (complete) PREMIERE
21 Nov.	Newcastle	*Beni Mora*
9 Dec.	London	*Two Songs Without Words*
31 Dec.	Chicago	THE PLANETS
1921		
11 Feb.	Cambridge	*The Hymn of Jesus*
15 Feb.	Leicester	*The Hymn of Jesus*
27 Feb.	Birmingham	*Beni Mora*
? March	Oxford	*Two Songs Without Words*
5 March	Newcastle	*The Hymn of Jesus*
8 March	York	*The Hymn of Jesus*
13 March	Chester	*Two Songs Without Words*
		Short Festival *Te Deum*
		The Djinn (from *The Sneezing Charm*)
20 May	London	*Japanese Suite*
31 May	Chicago	THE PLANETS
12 June	Oxford	*The Hymn of Jesus*
14 June	London	THE PLANETS
23 June	London	*Savitri*
		Choral *Hymns from the Rig Veda III*/1, 2, 4
17 Aug.	London	THE PLANETS (M, S, J)
8 Sep.	Hereford	*The Hymn of Jesus*
11 Sep.	Birmingham	*The Hymn of Jesus*
18 Sep.	London	THE PLANETS (M, S, Me, J)
7 Oct.	Brighton	THE PLANETS (M, S, J)
8 Oct.	London	THE PLANETS (M, S, Me, J)
13 Oct.	Bournemouth	THE PLANETS (M, S, J)
27 Oct.	London	*Beni Mora*
28 Oct.	Geneva	*Beni Mora*
7 Nov.	London	THE PLANETS
27 Nov.	London	*Beni Mora*
5 Dec.	Glyndebourne	*Beni Mora*

Appendix 2

Comparison of tempos in selected recordings of The Planets

Concerning the chart

The recordings used in the comparison chart were chosen with an eye toward variety of tempo markings, while trying to cover the full recording history of *The Planets*. The collection includes English, continental and American orchestras and conductors. Inclusion here is not meant to convey a judgment of quality; rather, the main purpose of the chart is to demonstrate the range of tempos used by conductors in their interpretation of musical character. The points within the music used for comparison were chosen following those used by Imogen in her listing of tempos and timings for her father's 1922–4 recordings (found in the facsimile score [Faber, 1974]). Some of her points were not used here, if they provided no interesting comparisons (*Venus*: m. 60, m. 85), and I added some which provided more interpretive details (*Mercury*: m. 83, m. 157; *Jupiter*: m. 226). As Imogen states in her remarks, many of the tempos are approximations (especially in the slow movements), due to expressive license. Tempo variance of two points either way should be considered equivalent. The tempos listed for the Holst recording are based on my own measurements and vary, sometimes significantly, from Imogen's list.

Concerning the Holst recording, Imogen states that the performance sounds hurried but that the tempos are not really much faster than those used by the composer in concert. In fact, the Holst tempos for the faster movements are surpassed on the chart only once: in *Jupiter*/234, a transitional passage. The chart demonstrates a wide variety of approaches to tempo. Sometimes a conductor will take one section of a movement slower than Holst did, but the next section will be faster than Holst's (compare Solti and Holst in *Venus*). The range of variance at specific points in the chart is sometimes small (*Venus*/1 = 12; *Jupiter*/108 = 10); but the widest variance is quite large (*Mars*/1 = 38; *Neptune*/50 = 54).

The chart

		Holst	Boult	Haitink	Bernstein	Marriner	Solti	Ozawa	Previn
Mars									
1	♩ =	172	166	134	172	142	170	160	170
96	𝅗𝅥 =	86	60	60	80	62	72	76	62
110	♩ =	172	160	136	170	140	164	156	164
Venus									
1	♩ =	62	54	54	50	54	52	54	54
32	♩ =	82	68	72	60	84	86	70	70
53	♩ =	100	78	72	64	86	80	72	68
94	♩ =	50	52	56	48	60	56	58	50
116	♩ =	52	54	58	52	72	60	60	54
Mercury									
1	♩. =	86	76	80	78	76	86	72	78
83	♩. =	82	78	74	78	74	78	70	78
157	♩. =	86	76	78	78	76	80	72	78
Jupiter									
1	♩ =	144	118	118	130	118	128	124	128
65	♩ =	144	122	128	136	124	128	128	132
108	♩ =	55	45	52	48	48	52	48	50
156	♩ =	152	148	138	146	134	152	134	144
194	♩ =	90	62	64	55	64	72	58	70
226	♩ =	72	56	58	52	60	68	62	68
234	♩ =	136	128	144	146	134	152	126	144
305	♩ =	146	130	140	120	124	136	130	136
348	𝅗𝅥 =	76	56	64	66	64	72	64	60
388	♩ =	76	56	58	54	60	68	68	62
Saturn									
1	♩ =	80	70	52	66	66	62	50	64
28	♩ =	76	74	64	78	84	70	72	72
50	♩ =	72	64	56	62	70	54	62	62
83	♩ =	120	108	96	138	124	114	116	88
105	𝅗𝅥 =	76	62	58	48	64	54	54	60
Uranus									
9	♩. =	116	92	106	118	118	120	112	108
222	♩ =	55	72	60	58	55	52	64	68
239	♩ =	55	66	64	70	70	55	64	66
Neptune									
1	♩ =	76	64	58	54	68	68	54	62
50	♩ =	120	102	106	66	98	90	72	82

Recordings used in the chart

Holst, London Symphony Orchestra, 1922–4, Pearl CD9417

Boult, Vienna State Opera Orchestra, c. 1960, MCA MCAD2-9813A

Haitink, London Philharmonic Orchestra, 1970, Philips 6500-072

Bernstein, New York Philharmonic Orchestra, 1973, CBS MYT 37226

Marriner, Concertgebouw Orchestra, 1978, Philips 9500-425

Solti, London Philharmonic Orchestra, 1979, London 425152-2

Ozawa, Boston Symphony Orchestra, 1979, Philips 416456-2

Previn, Royal Philharmonic Orchestra, 1986, Telarc CD80133

Notes

Introduction

1 Bax, *Ideas and People*, pp. 53–4.
2 See Leonard Ratner, *Classic Music*. Two good discussions of single pieces can be found in Leo Treitler, "History, criticism and Beethoven's Ninth Symphony," and Anthony Newcomb, "Once more between absolute and program music: Schumann's Second Symphony." Newcomb also points out that not all audiences had problems with this music, and that interpreting symphonic music in a semi-programmatic way became the basis for a school of critical thought in the latter part of the century.
3 This is my interpretation of the discussion in Carl Dahlhaus, "Issues in composition," in *Between Romanticism and Modernism*.
4 David Michael Hertz, *The Tuning of the Word*, pp. 32–55. On the aesthetic relationship between music and literature in Symbolist theory, see Chapter 6.
5 On Debussy, see James A. Hepokoski, "Formulaic openings in Debussy," and David Michael Hertz, *The Tuning of the Word*. For an aesthetic connection made by music critics between Holst and his French contemporaries, see Michael Short, *Gustav Holst*, p. 102.
6 For an excellent introduction to Holst's rhetorical method and musical language as well as full-scale analyses of many of his orchestral works, see Richard Greene, *Gustav Holst and a Rhetoric of Musical Character*.
7 Gustav Holst, "The mystic, the philistine and the artist."

1 Holst and the two Londons

1 But see "Vaughan Williams's talk on Parry and Stanford," in Ursula Vaughan Williams and Imogen Holst, *Heirs and Rebels*, pp. 94–5, for a discussion of Brahms as radical and progressive.
2 The fortnight chosen is busier than most, but it demonstrates the level of musical activity to which London could raise itself. It also has a larger than normal proportion of English works included.
3 Imogen Holst, *Gustav Holst*, p. vii.
4 For a full and lively discussion of these various popular styles see Ronald Pearsall, *Edwardian Popular Music*.
5 From a letter to Edwin Evans (29 January 1911), quoted in Imogen Holst, *Thematic Catalogue*, p. 103.
6 Imogen Holst, *Gustav Holst*, pp. 32–5.
7 Compare these comments on the third movement, *In the Street of the Ouled Nails*, quoted in Short, *Gustav Holst*, p. 100: "We do not ask for Biskra dancing girls in Langham Palace"; but, "On first hearing, this movement appears wholly bizarre, but a better acquaintance with it reveals great power and much striking beauty."
8 Short, *Gustav Holst*, p. 102.
9 Bax, *Ideas and People*, p. 54.

93

10 See particularly letters 9, 10, and 11 in Ursula Vaughan Williams and Imogen Holst, *Heirs and Rebels*, pp. 10–23.

11 Imogen Holst, *Gustav Holst*, p. 41.

12 For a discussion of Mahler's rhetoric and its reception by early audiences, see, for instance, Peter Franklin, *Mahler: Symphony No. 3*, pp. 26–33.

13 Mary Grierson, *Donald Francis Tovey*, pp. 217–19.

14 Scott Goddard, "An original genius," *Radio Times*, 51/654 (10 April 1936), quoted in Short, *Gustav Holst*, p. 186.

15 Dyneley Hussey on Holst in *Landmark* (February 1928), as discussed in Short, *Gustav Holst*, p. 214.

2 Genesis

1 Bax, *Ideas and People*, pp. 60–1.

2 Short, *Gustav Holst*, pp. 118–19.

3 "Farben" is the German word for color, and was used by Schoenberg as the title for the third movement of his *Five Pieces for Orchestra*. *Klangfarben* refers to Schoenberg's orchestral concept in the movement: shifting timbral combinations, serving as the primary musical content.

4 Ursula Vaughan Williams and Imogen Holst, *Heirs and Rebels*, pp. 62–3.

5 The manuscript is held at The Bodleian Library (MS Mus.b. 18/1–7). It was published in facsimile by Faber Ltd. in 1974.

6 For a full analysis and commentary on *A Somerset Rhapsody* see Richard Greene, *Gustav Holst and a Rhetoric of Musical Character*, Chapter 4.

7 For example: *Manchester Guardian* (11 October 1920), *Musical Opinion* (November 1920), *Musical News and Herald* (22 October 1921). One wonders, along with the reviewers, if Holst intended this symphonic concept, as he often conducted excerpt performances and, presumably, chose the movements to be played.

8 The lack of a material basis for such comparisons did not keep hostile reviewers from suggesting a clumsy plagiarism on Holst's part. These unfounded allegations prompted a response from Richard Capell who, in "Gustav Holst" in *Music & Letters*, 8/4 (October 1927), pp. 73–82, pointed out that parallels between Holst and other composers were of the same type as those between the chromaticism of Elgar and Wagner's *Parsifal*. They were part of the development of a musical tradition. Holst's usage, he maintained, was always personal and informed by the central idea of his composition.

9 Imogen Holst, *Gustav Holst*, p. 83.

3 Reception

1 This is not to suggest that Holst's critics were cowardly; it was a common practice for music critics in the press to remain anonymous.

2 *The Mirror of Music*, as quoted in Short, *Gustav Holst*, pp. 118–19.

3 Robert Hull, "Gustav Holst," in *English Review*, no. 50 (March 1930), pp. 369–74. Bernard van Dieren, "Stereoscopic views: 3. Gustav Holst," in *Dominant*, 1/12 (December 1928), pp. 13–20. Francis Toye, "Studies in English music: 7. Arnold Bax and Gustav Holst," in *The Listener* 6/133 (29 July 1931), p. 184. All are quoted in Short, *Gustav Holst*, pp. 264–5 and 339–41.

4 The character plots (1): *Mars* to *Mercury*

1 From the Herbert Thompson Collection, The University of Leeds, Brotherton Library, MS 361/148, 23 July [1922].

2 *Glasgow Herald*, 8 February 1926.
3 In some recorded performances, for example that of Seiji Ozawa and the Boston Symphony Orchestra, the timpani are brought to the foreground immediately, which shifts the sound to a more military one. While iconically effective, it does not honor the marking in the score.
4 *The Music of Gustav Holst*, p. 32.
5 *Gustav Holst*, p. 394.
6 Short, *Gustav Holst*, p. 123.
7 In a slow performance of *Mars*, such as Bernard Haitink's recording for Philips, a more noble character is felt. The ostinato is more of a solemn processional, and the overtly tonal and major-key passages are suffused with a human warmth. The sense of power and strength is positive rather than negative or sinister. However, Holst's marking and his own performances are much faster. See Appendix 2 for a comparison of performance tempos.
8 Emphasis is mine. The program notes are unattributed but it is unlikely that they were written by the composer. In the letter to Herbert Thompson quoted earlier (concerning notes for a later performance) Holst said "please add [program notes] if you think fit," but he made it clear that he did not like program notes and would not help the critic in writing them. A more likely candidate for the set in question is Eric Blom who was writing for Queen's Hall at that time. This is the first mention of a "hero" undergoing the psychological experience embodied by the music, representing the music specifically as a *human* experience.
9 *The Music of Gustav Holst*, p. 34.
10 Michael Short (*Gustav Holst*, p. 126) states that *Venus* reproduces the opening of Holst's *A Vigil of Pentecost* (1914, unpublished). Neither Short's *Centenary Documentation* nor Imogen Holst's *Thematic Catalogue* list performances, and Holst may well have had no program from this piece to transfer to *Venus*.
11 Michael Short traces this texture, particularly the celesta, to Schoenberg's *Five Pieces for Orchestra*. There is no metaphor correlation, only a technical one, and the texture here is as close to Elgar's orchestral version of *Salut d'amour* as it is to Schoenberg.
12 The University of Leeds, Brotherton Library, MS 361/147, 7 April [1922].
13 Published by Hawkes & Sons, London, 1925. For a discussion see Short, *Gustav Holst*, p. 132. There was perhaps some private association here for Holst, though it would be lost to the listener, since the *Japanese Suite* was seldom performed.

5 The character plots (2): *Jupiter* to *Neptune*

1 Imogen Holst, *Gustav Holst*, p. 81.
2 This and the following comments are found in Imogen Holst, *The Music of Gustav Holst*, pp. 36–8; Short, *Gustav Holst*, p. 129; and Edmund Rubbra, *Gustav Holst*, p. 22.
3 See Chapter 6 for a more detailed discussion of this theme.
4 Imogen Holst, *The Music of Gustav Holst*, p. 49.
5 Short, *Gustav Holst*, pp. 119–20 and 155–9
6 *The Music of Gustav Holst*, pp. 39–40

6 On becoming *The Planets*: the overall design

1 Adrian Boult commented at one time, with reference to the general public, that "when they are being given a totally new language like that, 30 minutes of it is as much as they can take in, and I am quite sure that 90% if not 95% of people only listen to one moment after another, and never think of music as a whole at all." (From a letter to Vally Lasker, quoted in Short, *Gustav Holst*, p. 170.)
2 This description of Holst's "personal" style could apply to Debussy and Stravinsky as well. A similarity between some of Holst's orchestral works (particularly *Beni Mora* and *The Phantastes*) and Stravinsky's early ballets was discussed in reviews, sometimes with a preference

stated for Holst. In general, there is a naiveté and rough-finished quality in Holst, which fit with his folk-orientation, setting his music apart from these other composers.

3 The *tutti/fff* orchestration enhances this fact.

Epilogue

1 Two additions to the literature after Short's study are E. L. Macan, *An Analytical Survey and Comparative Study of the Music of Ralph Vaughan Williams and Gustav Holst, c. 1910–1935* (Ph.D. diss., Claremont Graduate School, 1991), which includes a discussion of general theoretical properties of *Mars, Saturn*, and *Neptune*; and Richard Greene, *Orchestral Music of Gustav Holst: Musical Language and Rhetorical Method*, Chapter 5: 'The Planets' (Ph.D. diss., University of Leeds, 1992; forthcoming, under the title *Gustav Holst and a Rhetoric of Musical Character*, from Garland Publishing, Inc., New York).

2 On the concept of complex-tonality, see Greene, *Gustav Holst and a Rhetoric of Musical Character*.

3 T. F. Arnold, *Joseph Haydn. Seine kurze Biographie und aesthetische Darstellung seiner Werke* (Erfurt: J. C. Mueller, 1810), pp. 101–2, as translated by Mark Evan Bonds in his book, *Wordless Rhetoric: Musical Form and the Metaphor of the Oration* (Cambridge, MA: Harvard University Press, 1991), p. 138.

Select bibliography

Bax, Clifford. *Ideas and People*. London: Dickson, 1936

Dahlhaus, Carl. *Between Romanticism and Modernism: Four Studies in the Music of the Later Nineteenth Century*. Los Angeles and Berkeley: The University of California Press, 1974

Franklin, Peter. *Mahler: Symphony No. 3*. Cambridge: Cambridge University Press, 1991

Greene, Richard. "*Country Song*: an example of Gustav Holst's rhetorical method," *The Music Review*, 50/3–4 (August/November 1989), pp. 240–64

"A musico-rhetorical outline of Holst's *Egdon Heath*," *Music & Letters*, 73/2 (May 1992), pp. 244–67

Gustav Holst and a Rhetoric of Musical Character: Language and Method in Selected Orchestral Works. New York: Garland Publishing Inc., 1994

Grierson, Mary. *Donald Francis Tovey: A Biography Based on Letters*. London: Oxford University Press, 1952

Hepokoski, James A. "Formulaic openings in Debussy," *19th Century Music*, 8/1 (Summer 1984), pp. 44–59

Hertz, David Michael. *The Tuning of the Word: The Musico-Literary Poetics of the Symbolist Movement*. Carbondale, IL: Southern Illinois University Press, 1987

Holst, Gustav. "The mystic, the philistine and the artist," *Quest*, 11/3 (April 1920), pp. 366–79; reprinted in Imogen Holst, *Gustav Holst*, 1969, pp. 194–204

The Planets (score). Ernst Eulenburg Ltd., 1985

Holst, Imogen. *Gustav Holst: A Biography*. 2nd edn London: Oxford University Press, 1969; 1st edn 1938

A Thematic Catalogue of Gustav Holst's Music. London: Faber Music Ltd., 1974

The Music of Gustav Holst (3rd edition revised), and Holst's Music Reconsidered. London: Oxford University Press, 1986

Howes, Frank. "Music," in Simon Nowell-Smith (ed.), *Edwardian England: 1901–1914*. Oxford: Oxford University Press, 1964, pp. 411–46

Marias, Julian. *The History of Philosophy*. New York: Dover, 1967

Marriott, Sir J. A. R. *Modern Britain, 1885–1932*. London: Methuen & Co., 1934

Matthews, Colin (ed.) [Holst]. *The Planets* (score). Ernst Eulenburg Ltd., 1985

Newcomb, Anthony. "Once more between absolute and program music: Schumann's Second Symphony," *19th Century Music*, 7/3 (April 1984), pp. 233–50

Pearsall, Ronald. *Edwardian Popular Music*. Rutherford: Fairleigh Dickinson University Press, 1975

Pirie, Peter J. *The English Musical Renaissance*. New York: St. Martin's Press, 1979

Ratner, Leonard. *Classic Music: Form, Expression and Style*. New York: Schirmer Books, 1980

Rubbra, Edmund. *Gustav Holst*. Monaco: Lyrebird Press, 1947

Gustav Holst: Collected Essays. London: Triad Press, 1974

Shore, Bernard. *Sixteen Symphonies*. London: Longmans, 1949

Short, Michael. *Gustav Holst: A Centenary Documentation*. London: White Lion Press, 1974

Gustav Holst: The Man and His Music. London: Oxford University Press, 1990

Treitler, Leo. "History, criticism and Beethoven's Ninth Symphony," *19th Century Music*, 3/3 (March 1980), pp. 193–210

Vaughan Williams, Ursula and Imogen Holst (eds.), *Heirs and Rebels: Letters Written to Each Other and Occasional Writings on Music by Gustav Holst and Ralph Vaughan Williams*. London: Oxford University Press, 1959; Reprinted Westport, CT: Greenwood Press, 1980

Index

Algeria 12
Arts Gazette 30, 34
astrology 14, 15, 18, 20, 36, 41, 42, 55
Athenaeum 34, 39

Bax, Clifford 2, 13, 18, 57
Beethoven, Ludwig van 3, 5, 10, 20, 21, 38, 70, 82, 84
Berlioz, Hector 20, 23, 64
Birmingham Gazette & Express 34
Birmingham Mail 34
Birmingham News 34
Birmingham Post 34
Blom, Eric 70

Capell, Richard 30, 35, 38, 84
Colles, H. C. 30
complex-tonality 85

Daily Chronicle 34
Daily Express 34
Daily Herald 34
Daily Mail 34, 35
Daily News 34
Daily Telegraph 34
Debussy, Claude 5, 6, 23, 24, 36, 64, 82
Dunton Green, L. 30, 32, 84

Ein Heldenleben 19, 24, 69
Elgar, Edward 1, 14, 26, 37, 69, 82
Evans, Edwin 30, 32, 37
Evening News 34
Evening Standard 34

folksong 12, 19, 21, 70, 72

Gardiner, Balfour 9, 10, 12, 13, 15, 28
Globe, The 32, 34, 35

Holbrooke, Josef 10

Holst, Gustav
  Compositions:
  A Fugal Concerto 17
  A Somerset Rhapsody 6, 12, 13, 19, 21
  Beni Mora 6, 11–13, 22, 38, 53, 69
  Choral Hymns from the Rig Veda 12, 13, 19, 20
  Dirge and Hymeneal 20, 27, 65
  Dirge for Two Veterans 19, 27
  Double Concerto 17, 64
  Egdon Heath 6, 7, 17, 38, 58, 83, 85
  Hammersmith 6, 9, 15, 64, 83
  Japanese Suite 27, 53
  Lyric Movement 6
  Nunc Dimittis 27
  Savitri 6, 20, 65
  Sita 12, 20
  The Choral Symphony 6
  The Cloud Messenger 5, 10, 13
  The Hymn of Jesus 16, 17, 28–30, 65, 83, 84
  The Mystic Trumpeter 5
  The Perfect Fool 29, 64, 84
  The Phantastes Suite 12, 13, 61–3
  Two Songs Without Words 11, 33
Holst, Imogen 12, 38, 43, 45, 48, 58, 62, 83, 84

Klangfarben 19, 22, 25, 65, 70, 78

L'Apprenti Sorcier 24, 36, 61, 63
Ladies' Field 34
Leo, Alan 1, 41–3, 47, 52, 61

Mahler, Gustav 14, 15, 20, 58, 84
Manchester Guardian 31, 34
metaphor 3, 5–7, 14, 40, 42, 46, 47, 51, 54, 58, 68, 69, 73, 80, 82–5
Monthly Musical Record 34
Morning Post 32, 34

Printed in the United Kingdom
by Lightning Source UK Ltd.
123346UK00001B/43-51/A